Progress Chart

W9-AUK-605

This chart lists the topics in the book. Once you have completed each page, stick a star in the correct box below.

Page	Topic	Star	Page	Topic	Star	Page	Topic	Star
2	**1** Write the number	☆	12	Can you remember?	☆	22	**10** Write the number	☆
3	**1** Write the word	☆	13	Can you remember?	☆	23	**10** Write the word	☆
4	**2** Write the number	☆	14	**6** Write the number	☆	24	Can you remember?	☆
5	**2** Write the word	★	15	**6** Write the word	☆	25	Can you remember?	☆
6	**3** Write the number	☆	16	**7** Write the number	☆	26	**11** and **12** Write the numbers	☆
7	**3** Write the word	☆	17	**7** Write the word	☆	27	**13** and **14** Write the numbers	☆
8	**4** Write the number	☆	18	**8** Write the number	☆	28	**15** and **16** Write the numbers	☆
9	**4** Write the word	★	19	**8** Write the word	☆	29	**17** and **18** Write the numbers	☆
10	**5** Write the number	☆	20	**9** Write the number	☆	30	**19** and **20** Write the numbers	☆
11	**5** Write the word	☆	21	**9** Write the word	☆	31	Can you remember?	☆

When you have completed
the progress chart in this book, fill in
the certificate at the back.

Math
made easy

Kindergarten - ages 5-6
Workbook

Author and Consultant
Su Hurrell

DORLING KINDERSLEY

Published by the Penguin Group
Penguin Group (USA) Inc., 375 Hudson Street, New York, New York 10014, U.S.A.
Penguin Books Ltd, Registered Offices: 80 Strand, London WC2R 0RL, England

First published in the United States by DK Publishing, Inc. in 2003
Reprinted 2004, 2008

Copyright © 2003 Dorling Kindersley Limited

Printed and bound in China by L. Rex Printing

12 13 14 15 14 13 12 11 10

013-MB994P-06/2001

LONDON • NEW YORK • SYDNEY • MOSCOW • DELHI

1

Write the number.

Count.

How many?

How many?

How many?

Copy the pattern.

0 ☐ 2 3 4 5 6 7 8 9 10

I

Write the word.

one one

Draw one spoon.   Draw one spoon.

Match.

0 ☐ 2 3 4 5 6 7 8 9 10

2

Write the number.

2 2 2 2 . . .

Count how many.

Copy the pattern.

0 1 ▢ 3 4 5 6 7 8 9 10

2

Write the word.

two   ˙˙˙˙˙˙

Draw two.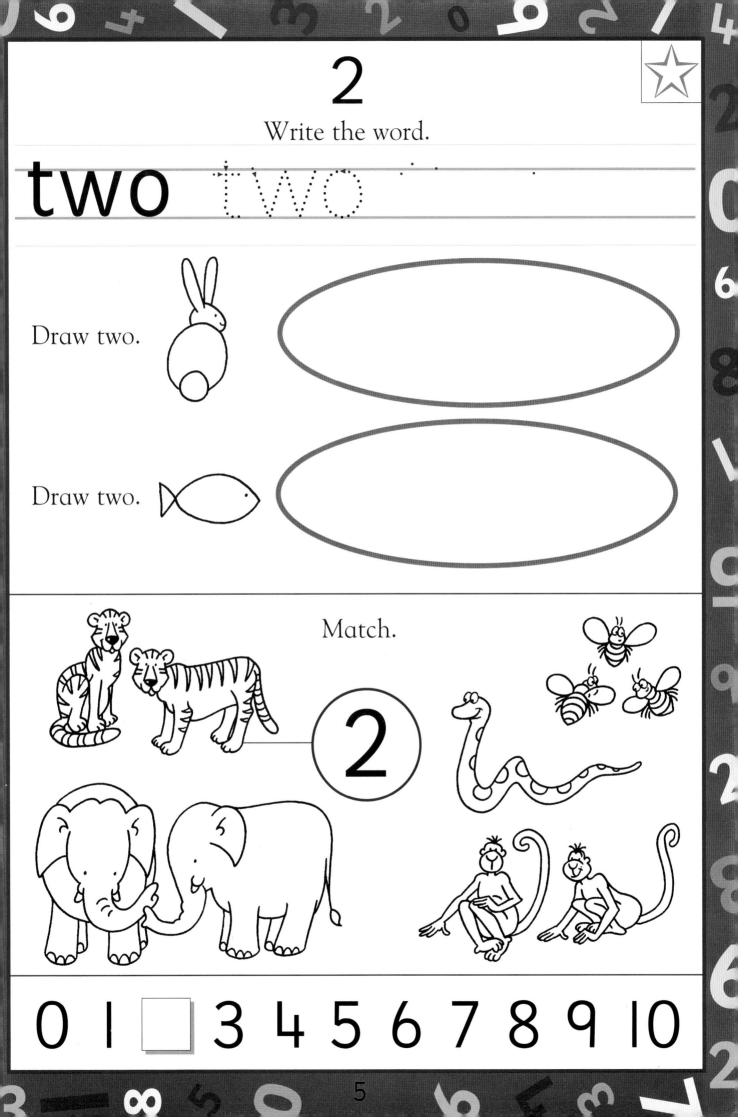

Draw two.

Match.

2

0 1 ☐ 3 4 5 6 7 8 9 10

3

Write the number.

3　3　3　3　.　.　.

Count how many.

Copy the pattern.

0 1 2 ☐ 4 5 6 7 8 9 10

3

Write the word.

three   three

Ring the sets of three.

Ring the number to match.

| 1 ②3 | 1 2 3 | 1 2 3 |

0 1 2 ☐ 4 5 6 7 8 9 10

4

Write the number.

4   4   4   4

Count how many sheep.

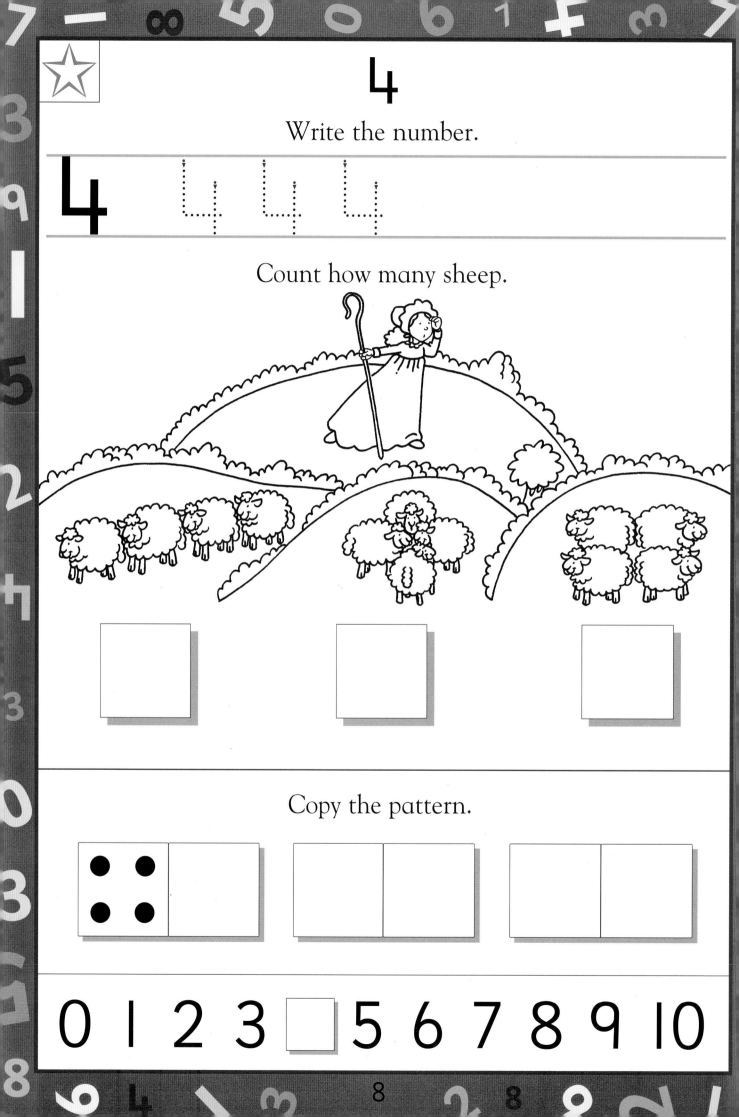

Copy the pattern.

4

Write the word.

four four

Match the sets of sheep to the field.

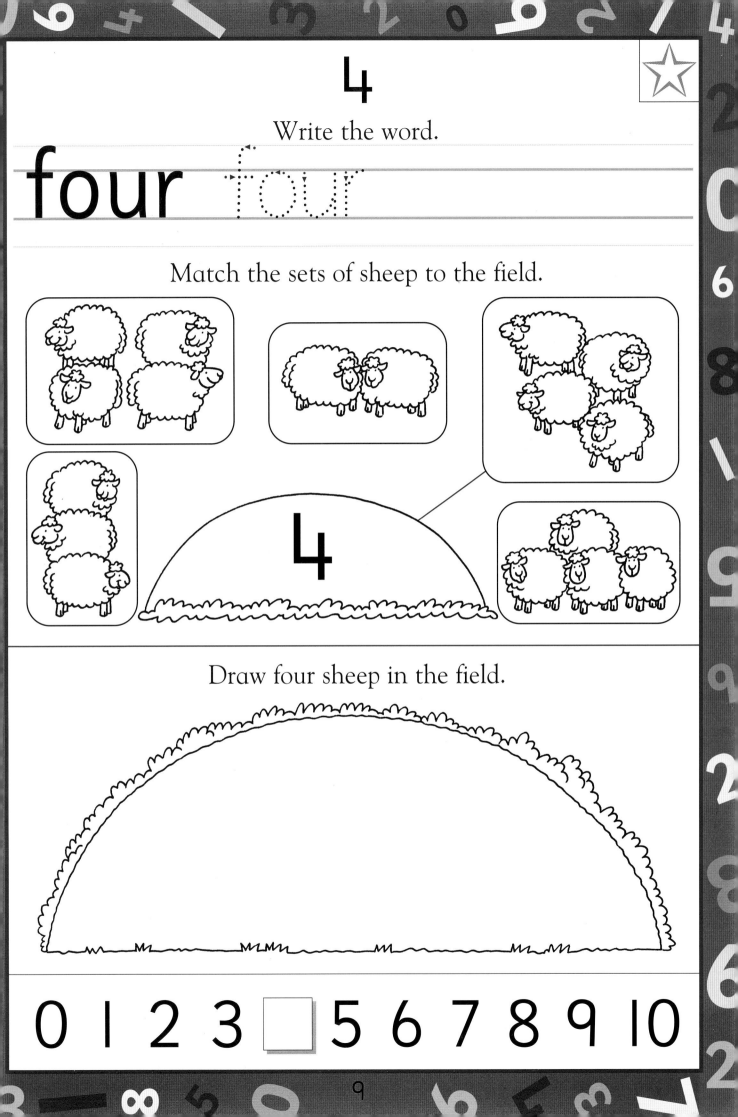

4

Draw four sheep in the field.

0 1 2 3 ☐ 5 6 7 8 9 10

5

Write the number.

5 5 5 5

Count how many.

Copy the pattern.

5

Write the word.

five ~~five~~

Count how many fish have five spots.

Draw five fish.

0 1 2 3 4 ☐ 6 7 8 9 10

Can you remember?

Write the numbers.

1 2 3 4 5

Count how many.

Can you remember?

Match the kites to the numbers.

Match the number to the nest.

1   2   3   4   5

0 □ □ □ □ □ 6 7 8 9 10

13

6

Write the number.

6 6 6 6

Count how many.

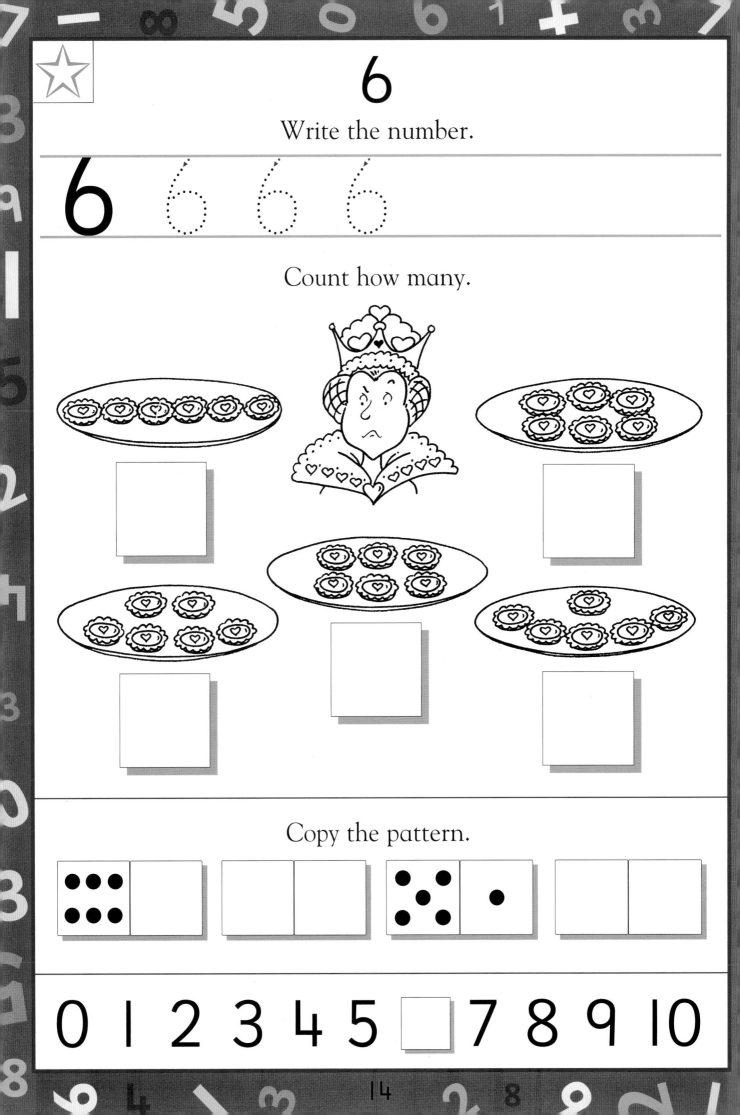

Copy the pattern.

0 1 2 3 4 5 ☐ 7 8 9 10

6

Write the word.

six six

Match the number to the plates of cookies.

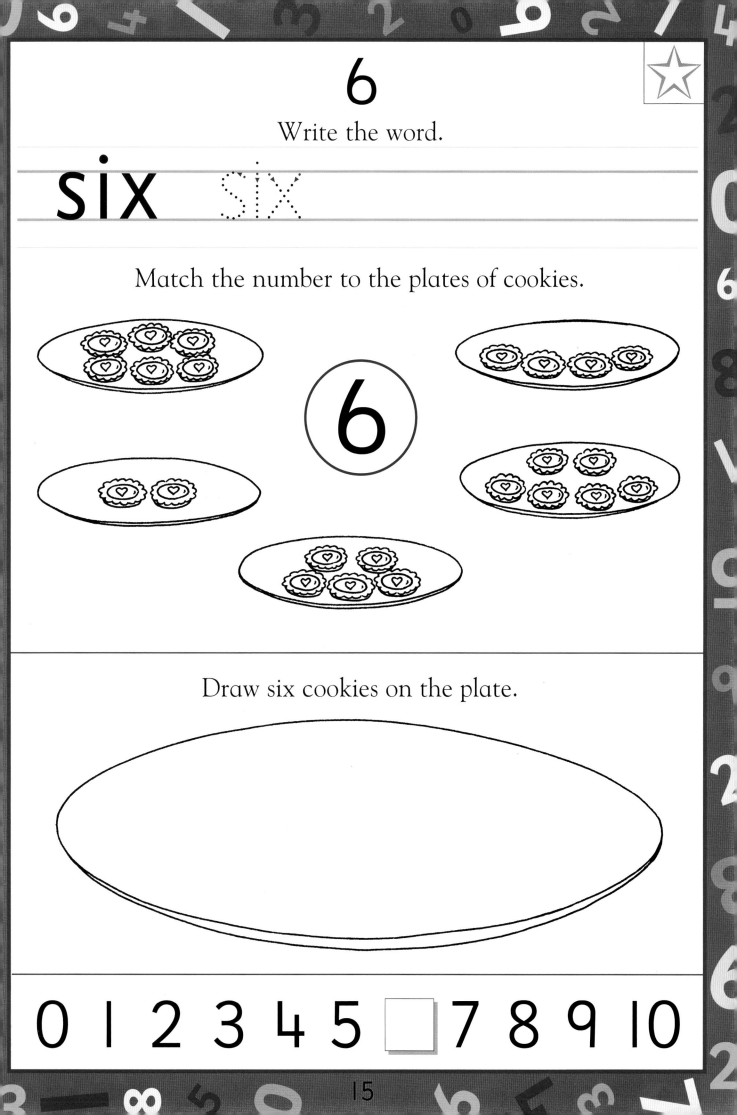

6

Draw six cookies on the plate.

0 1 2 3 4 5 ☐ 7 8 9 10

7

Write the number.

7

7 7 7

Count how many.

Copy the pattern.

0 1 2 3 4 5 6 [ ] 8 9 10

16

7

Write the word.

seven seven

Ring the number that matches.

1 2 3 ④ 5 6 7

1 2 3 4 5 6 7

1 2 3 4 5 6 7

1 2 3 4 5 6 7

1 2 3 4 5 6 7

Count how many sets have seven flowers.

0 1 2 3 4 5 6 ☐ 8 9 10

8

Write the number.

8 8 8 8

Count how many children.

Copy the pattern.

0 1 2 3 4 5 6 7 ☐ 9 10

8

Write the word.

eight eight

Write the numbers on the steps.

1

8

Write the number on the clock.

0 1 2 3 4 5 6 7 ☐ 9 10

9

Write the number.

9   9   9   9

Count how many stars.

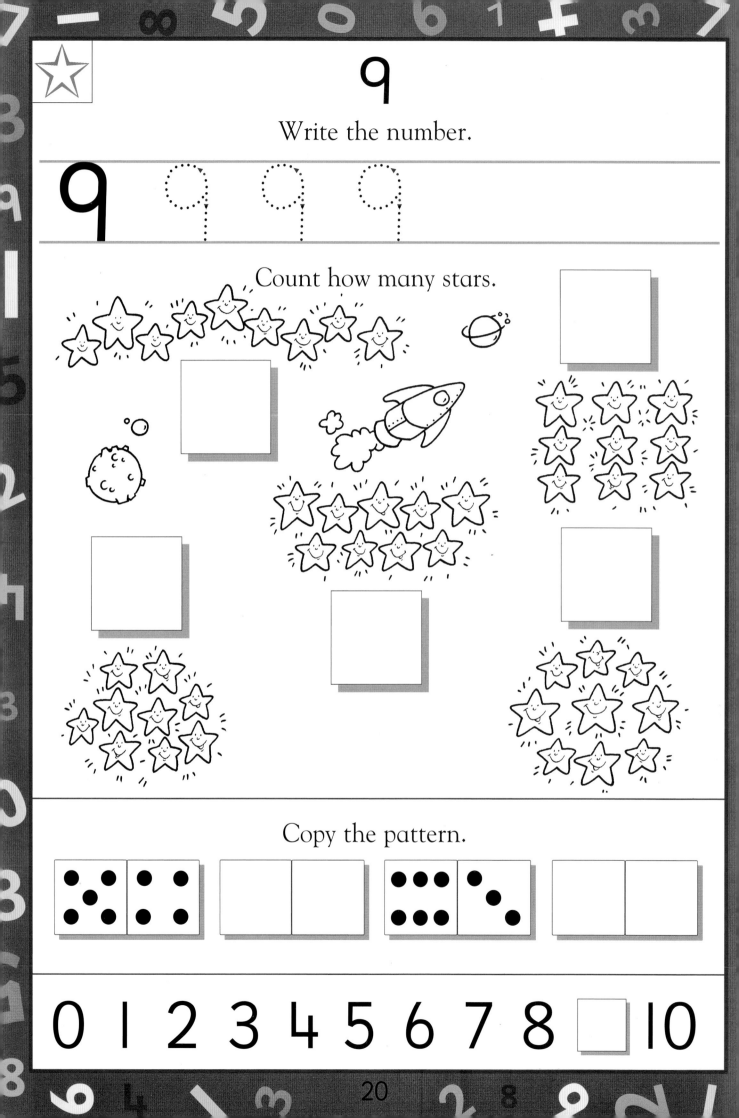

Copy the pattern.

0 1 2 3 4 5 6 7 8 ☐ 10

9

Write the word.

nine nine

Draw nine stars.

Match.

0 1 2 3 4 5 6 7 8 ☐ 10

10

Write the number.

10　10　10　10

Count how many.

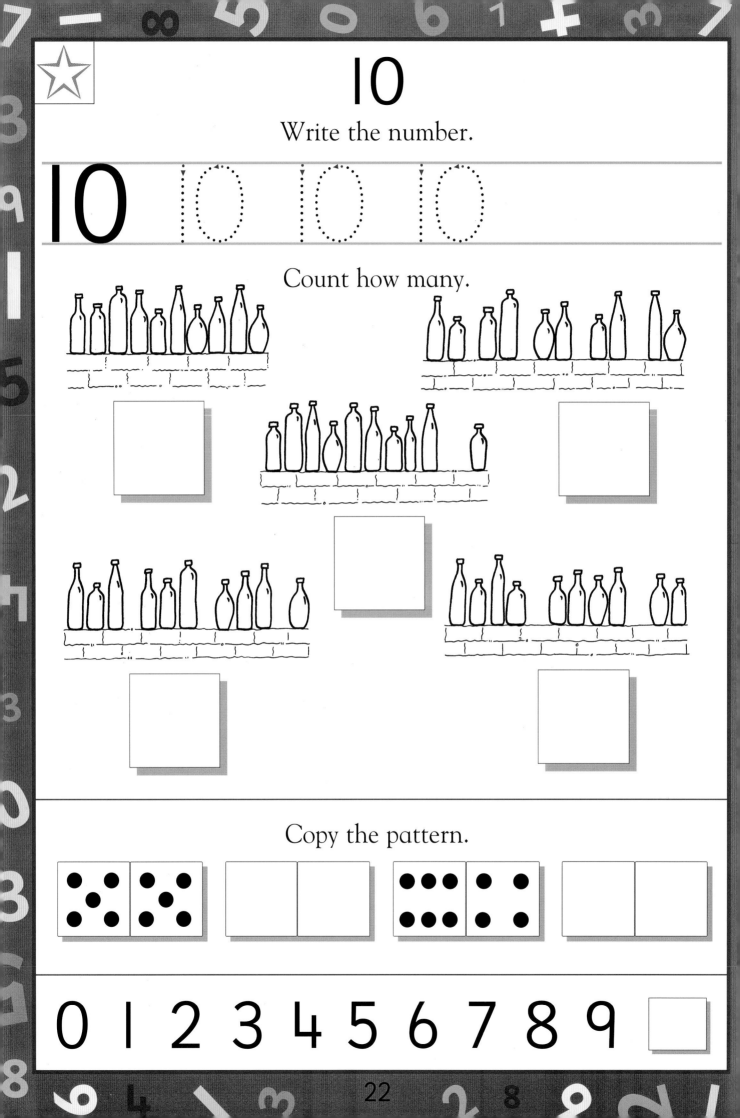

Copy the pattern.

0 1 2 3 4 5 6 7 8 9

10

Write the word.

ten ˙ten˙

Draw ten bottles on a wall.

Ring the number that matches.

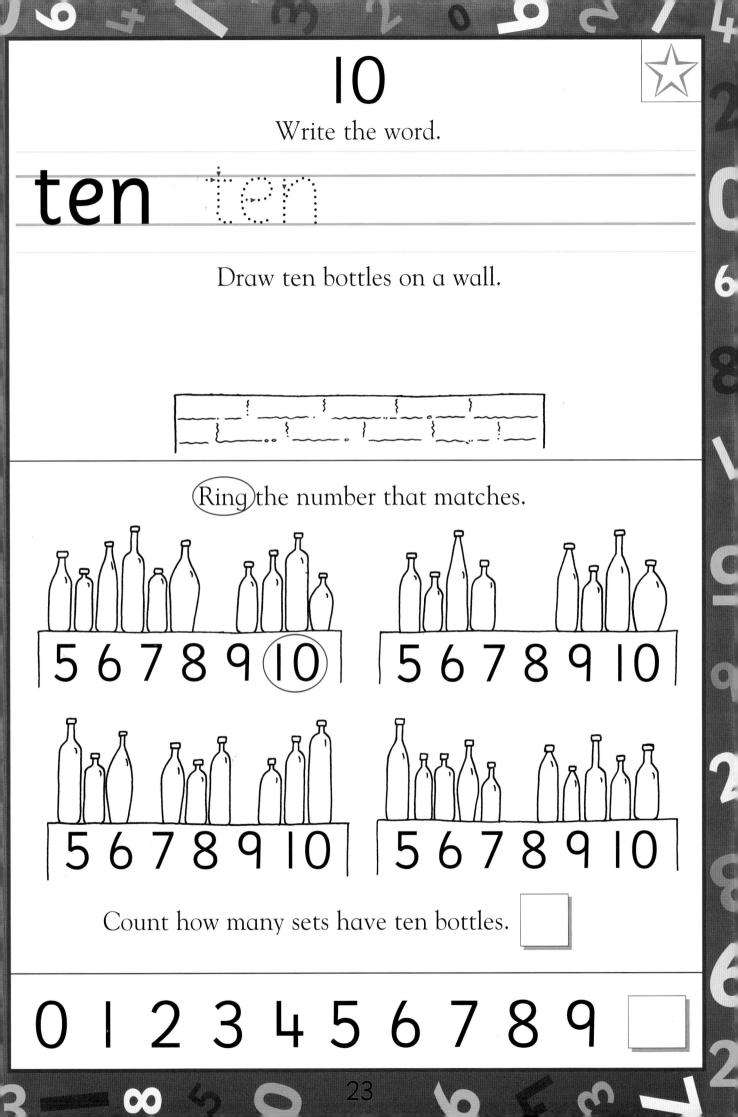

5 6 7 8 9 (10)

5 6 7 8 9 10

5 6 7 8 9 10

5 6 7 8 9 10

Count how many sets have ten bottles. ☐

0 1 2 3 4 5 6 7 8 9 ☐

Can you remember?

Write the numbers.

6   7   8   9   10

Match the hats to the teddy bears.

eight   six   ten   nine   seven

6   7   8   9   10

Count the buttons.

Count the buttons boxes.

0 1 2 3 4 5

Can you remember?

Connect the dots.

11 and 12

Write the numbers.

11 ¦¦   12 ¦2

Count how many.

Draw 11 balloons.

Draw 12 cup cakes.

10 ☐ ☐ 13 14 15 16 17 18 19 20

13 and 14

Write the numbers.

13 |3 14 |4

Count how many.

Draw 13 candies.

Draw 14 lollipops.

10 11 12 ☐ ☐ 15 16 17 18 19 20

15 and 16

Write the numbers.

15 ⁝5⁝   16 ⁝6⁝

Ring the number that matches.

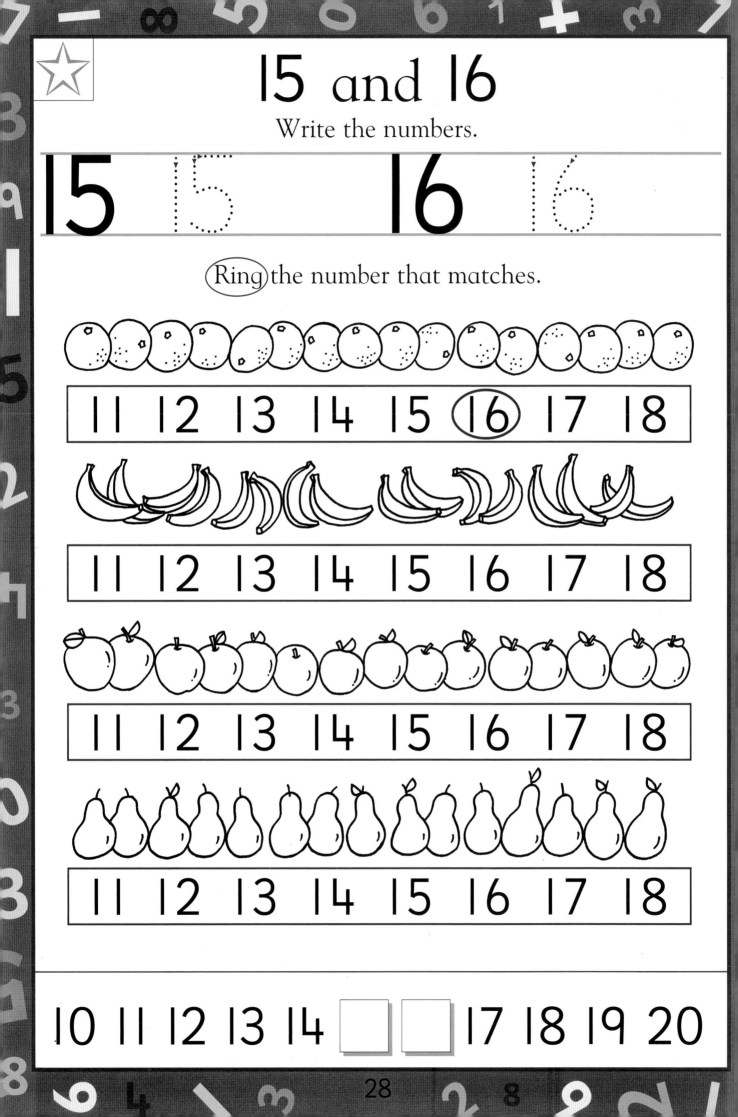

11 12 13 14 15 ⑯ 17 18

11 12 13 14 15 16 17 18

11 12 13 14 15 16 17 18

11 12 13 14 15 16 17 18

10 11 12 13 14 ☐ ☐ 17 18 19 20

17 and 18

Write the numbers.

17 17 18 18

Match the numbers to the sets.

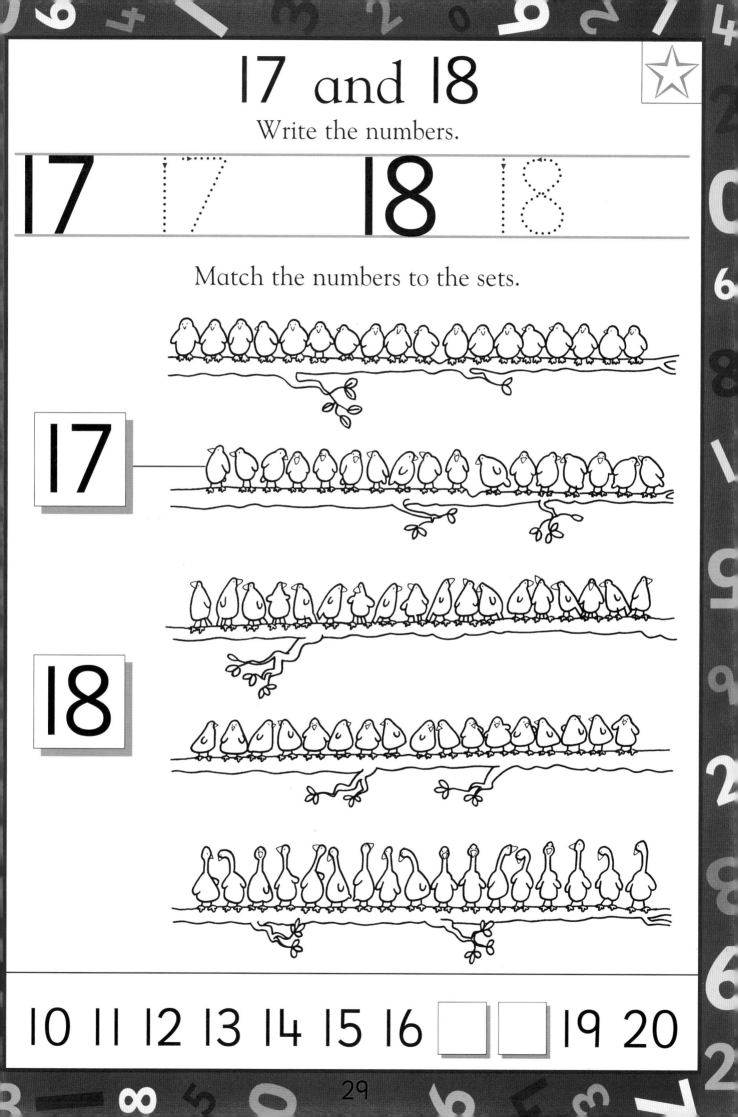

17

18

10 11 12 13 14 15 16 ☐ ☐ 19 20

19 and 20

Write the numbers.

19 19   20 20

Count how many.

10 11 12 13 14 15 16 17 18 ☐ ☐

Can you remember?

Write the missing numbers.

Can you remember?

Join the dots.

More than

Draw more beads.

Draw more bricks.

Draw more spots.

0 1 2 3 4 5 6 7 8 9 10

I more than

Match the circles. ✔ I more.

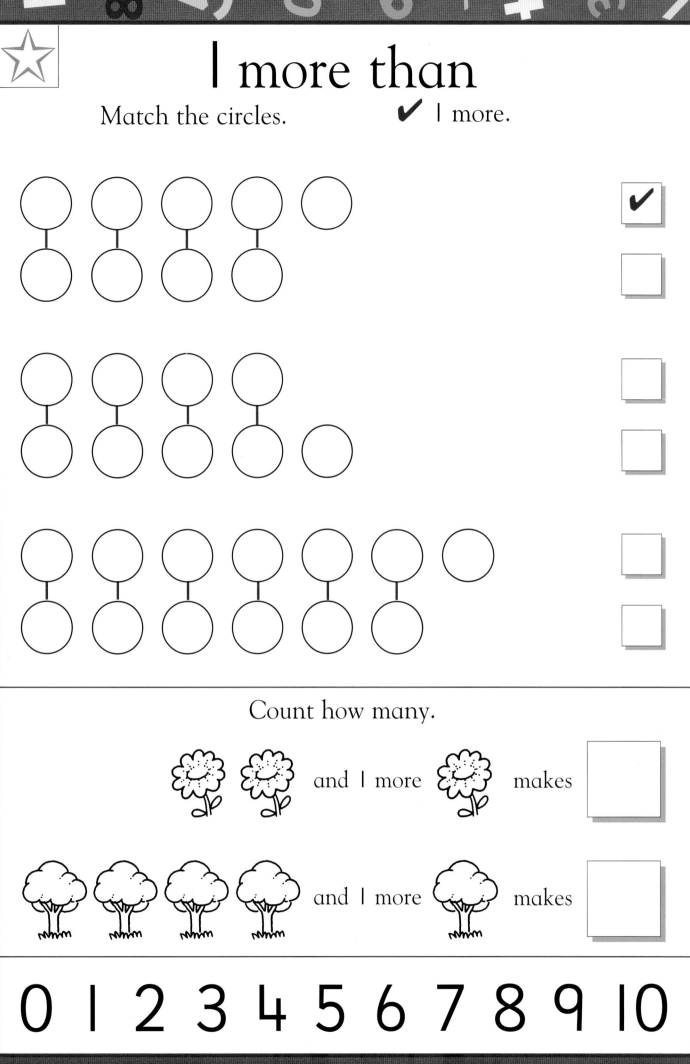

Count how many.

and I more makes [ ]

and I more makes [ ]

0 1 2 3 4 5 6 7 8 9 10

And 1 more

Draw 1 more.　　　　Count how many.

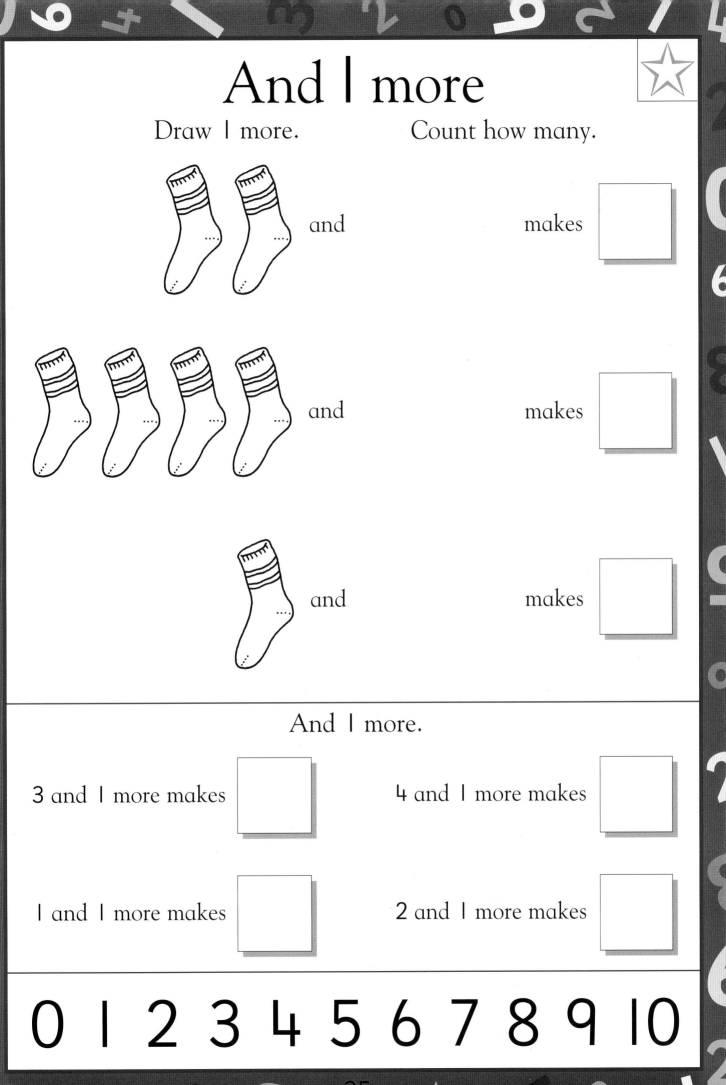

and　　　　makes

and　　　　makes

and　　　　makes

And 1 more.

3 and 1 more makes

4 and 1 more makes

1 and 1 more makes

2 and 1 more makes

0 1 2 3 4 5 6 7 8 9 10

2 more than

Match the hats. ✔ 2 more.

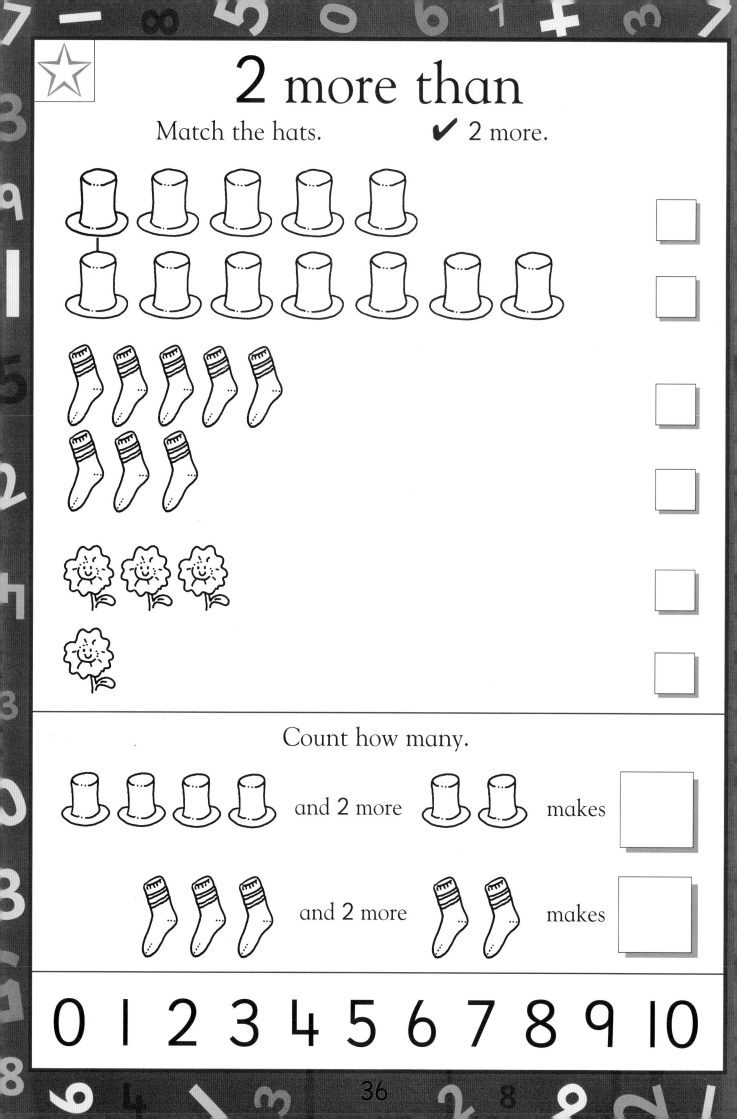

Count how many.

and 2 more makes

and 2 more makes

0 1 2 3 4 5 6 7 8 9 10

And 2 more

Draw 2 more.   Count how many.

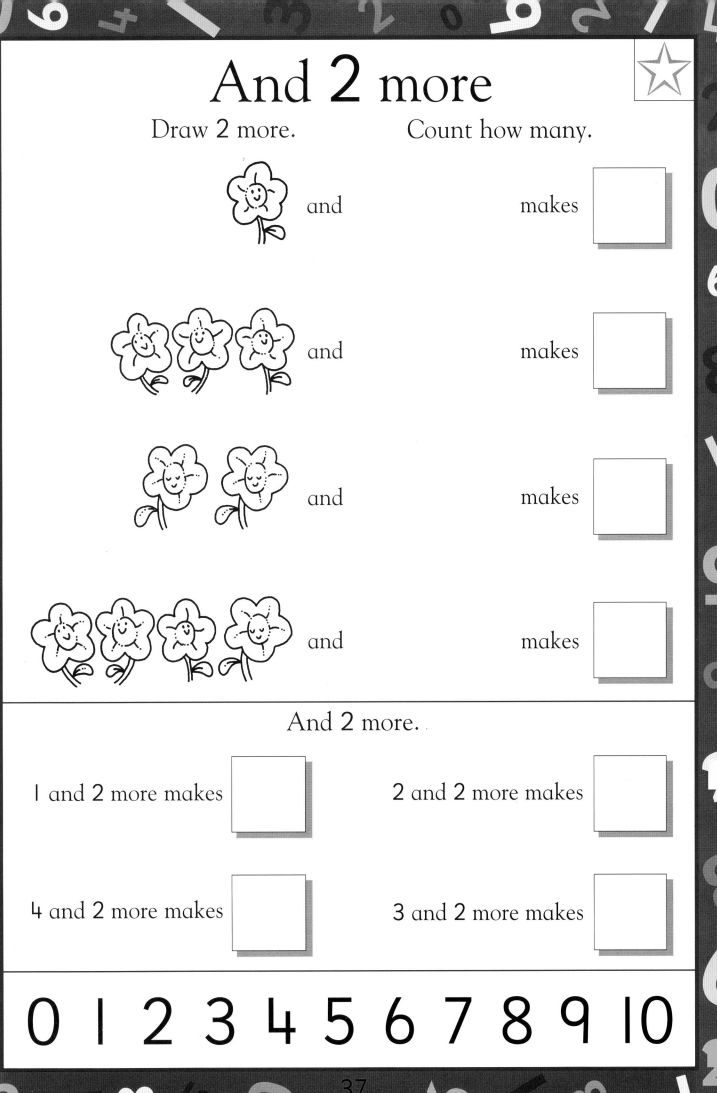

and _____ makes [ ]

and _____ makes [ ]

and _____ makes [ ]

and _____ makes [ ]

And 2 more.

1 and 2 more makes [ ]   2 and 2 more makes [ ]

4 and 2 more makes [ ]   3 and 2 more makes [ ]

0 1 2 3 4 5 6 7 8 9 10

☆

3 more than

Match the cakes. ✔ 3 more.

Count how many.

and 3 more ⬜⬜⬜ makes ⬜

and 3 more ⬜⬜⬜ makes ⬜

0 1 2 3 4 5 6 7 8 9 10

And 3 more

Draw 3 more.   Count how many.

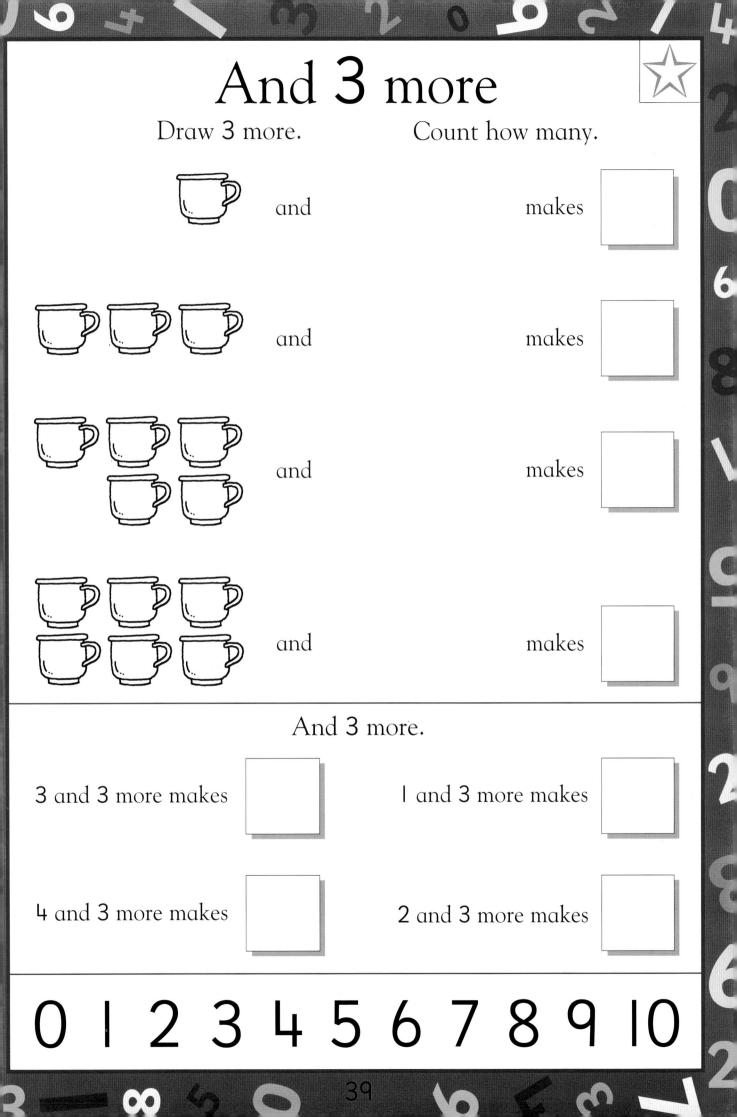

and   makes

and   makes

and   makes

and   makes

And 3 more.

3 and 3 more makes

1 and 3 more makes

4 and 3 more makes

2 and 3 more makes

0 1 2 3 4 5 6 7 8 9 10

4 more than

Match the buttons. ✔ 4 more.

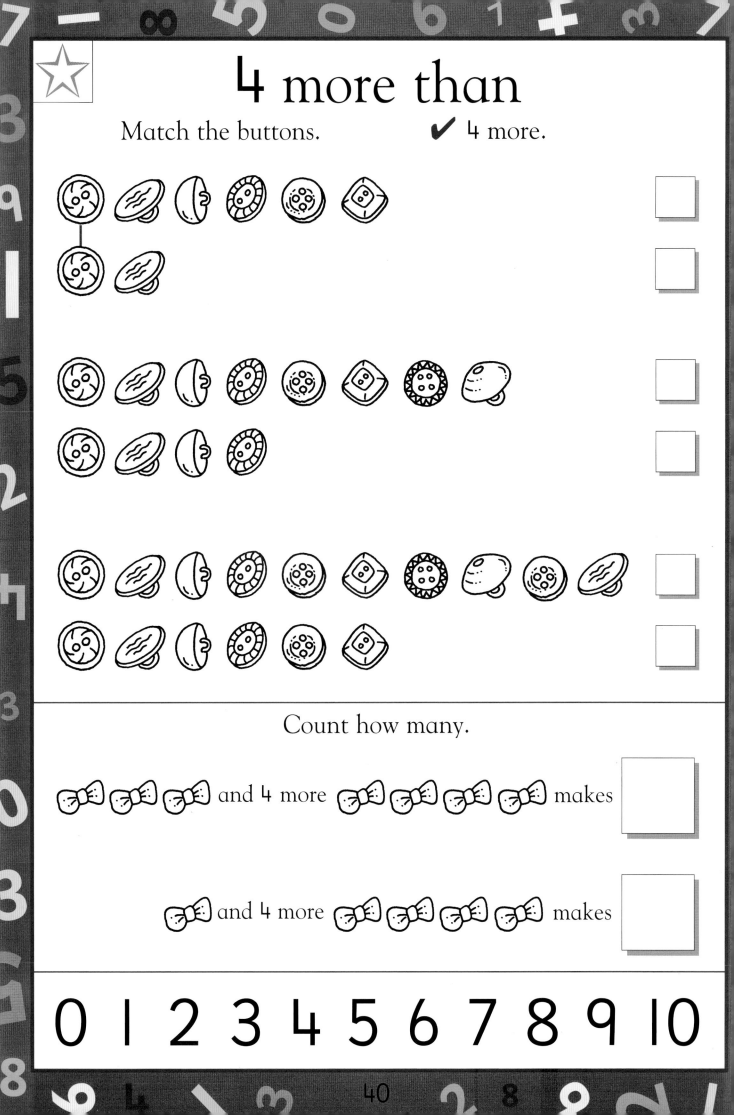

Count how many.

and 4 more makes

and 4 more makes

0 1 2 3 4 5 6 7 8 9 10

And 4 more

Draw 4 more.   Count how many.

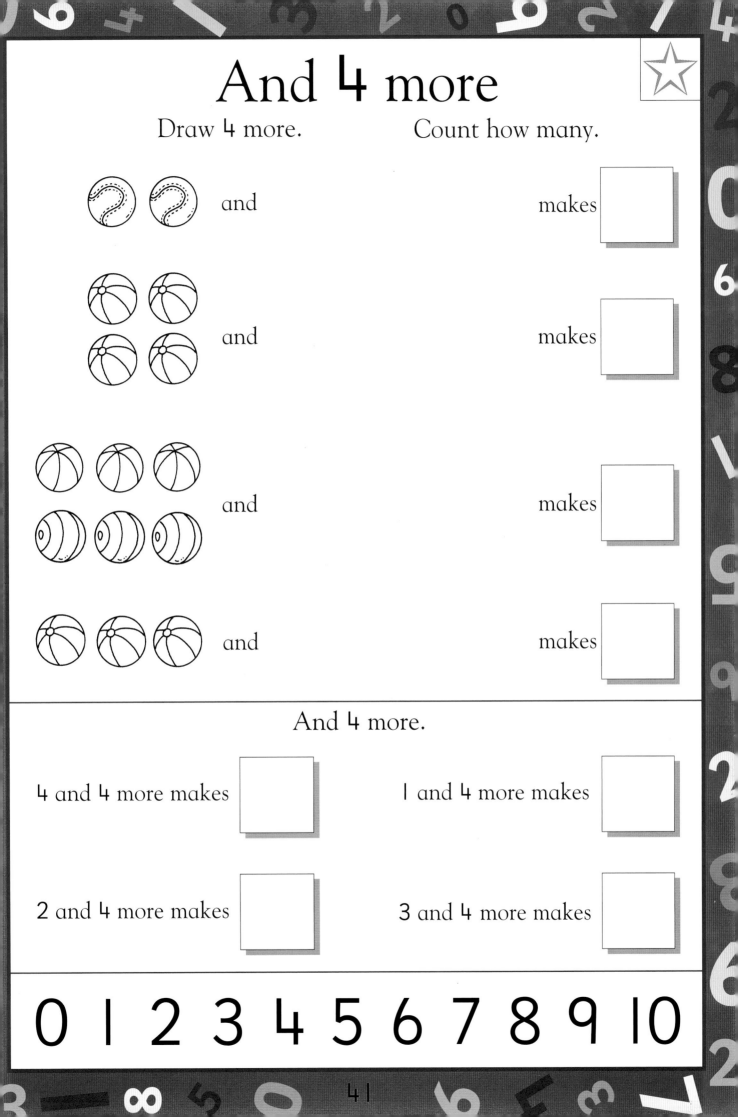

and _____ makes ☐

and _____ makes ☐

and _____ makes ☐

and _____ makes ☐

And 4 more.

4 and 4 more makes ☐   1 and 4 more makes ☐

2 and 4 more makes ☐   3 and 4 more makes ☐

0 1 2 3 4 5 6 7 8 9 10

5 more than

Match the shells.   ✔ 5 more.

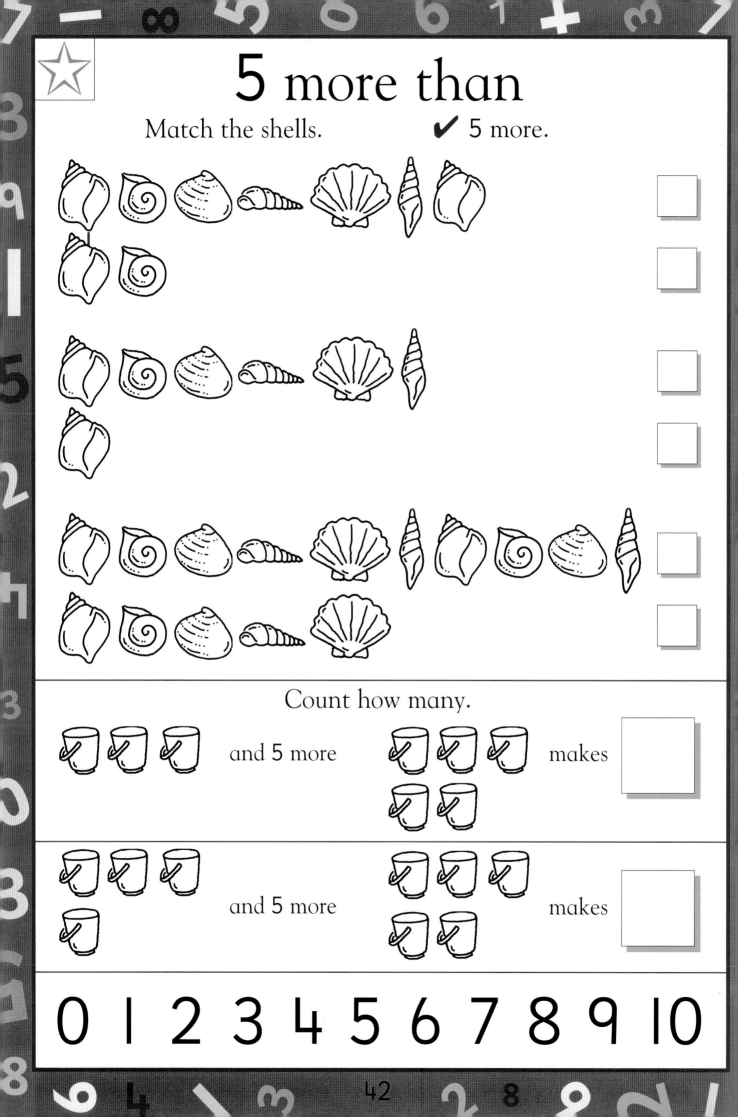

Count how many.

and 5 more ... makes

and 5 more ... makes

0 1 2 3 4 5 6 7 8 9 10

And 5 more

Draw 5 more.   Count how many.

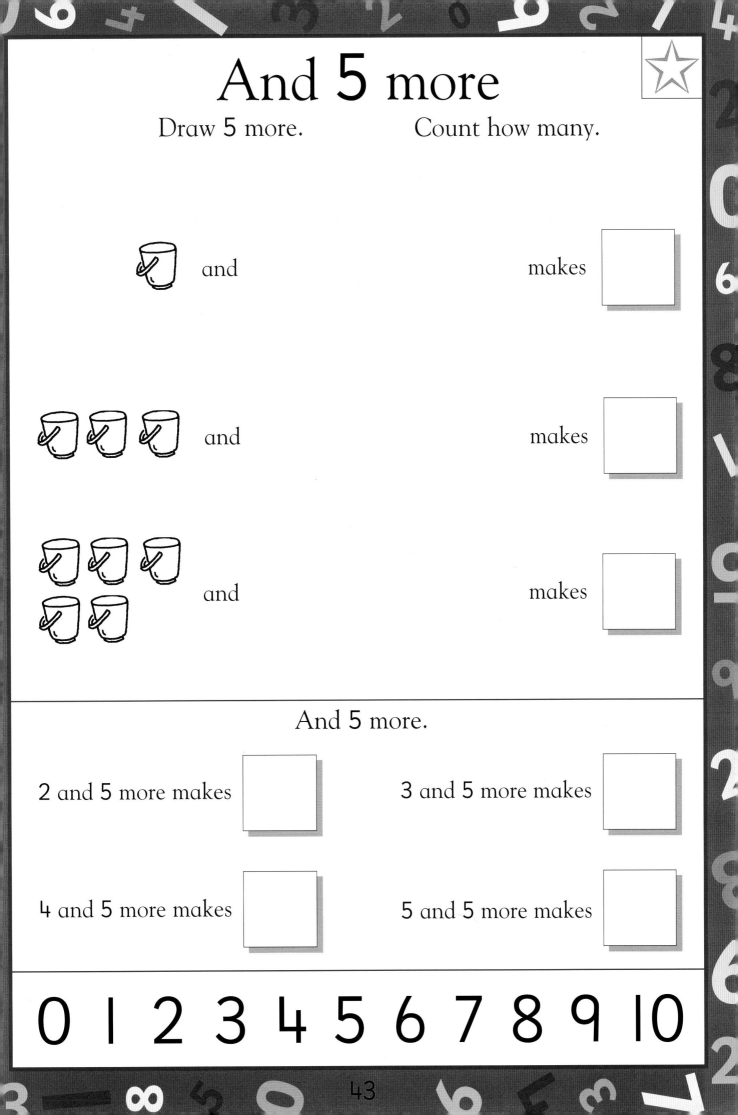

and   makes

and   makes

and   makes

And 5 more.

2 and 5 more makes

3 and 5 more makes

4 and 5 more makes

5 and 5 more makes

0 1 2 3 4 5 6 7 8 9 10

43

Count how many

○ and ○ ○ more makes

○ ○ and ○ ○ / ○ ○ more makes

○ ○ ○ and ○ more makes

○ ○ / ○ ○ and ○ ○ ○ more makes

○ ○ ○ / ○ ○ and ○ ○ more makes

○ ○ ○ and ○ ○ ○ more makes

○ ○ and ○ ○ more makes

○ ○ / ○ ○ and ○ ○ / ○ ○ more makes

○ ○ ○ and ○ ○ ○ / ○ ○ more makes

0 1 2 3 4 5 6 7 8 9 10

Count how many

1 and 1 more makes ☐

3 and 1 more makes ☐

3 and 2 more makes ☐

1 and 3 more makes ☐

2 and 1 more makes ☐

3 and 4 more makes ☐

2 and 5 more makes ☐

4 and 3 more makes ☐

2 and 3 more makes ☐

5 and 5 more makes ☐

4 and 4 more makes ☐

4 and 5 more makes ☐

3 and 5 more makes ☐

3 and 3 more makes ☐

0 1 2 3 4 5 6 7 8 9 10

Fewer than

Look. ✔ the tree with fewer apples.

☐ ☐

Look. ✔ the plate with fewer cup cakes.

☐ ☐

Look. ✔ the dog with fewer spots.

☐ ☐

Fewer

Draw fewer candies.

Draw fewer pennies.

Draw fewer eggs.

Draw fewer socks.

1 fewer than

Count how many. ✔ 1 fewer.

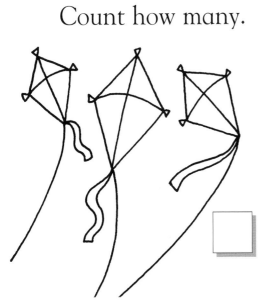

☐

☐

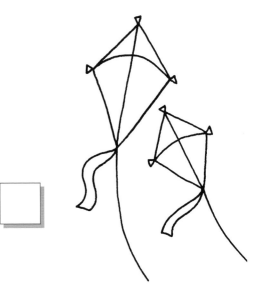

☐

☐

☐

☐

Take 1 away

✘ 1 out. Count how many are left.

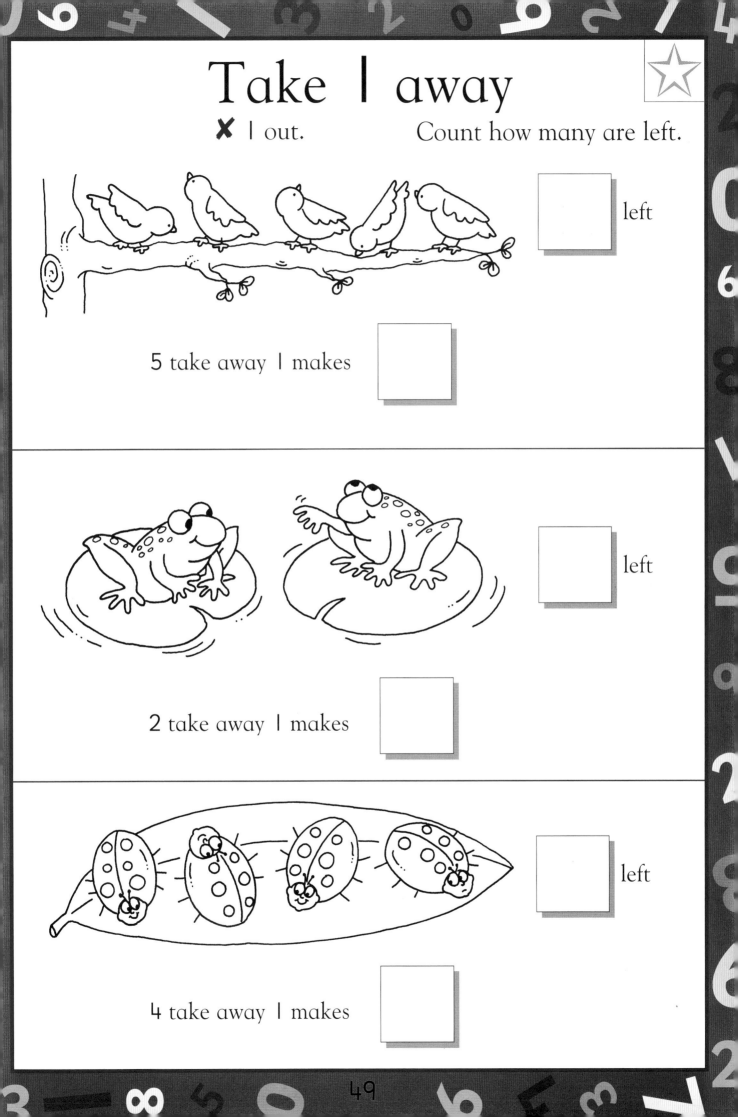

☆

5 take away 1 makes ☐

☐ left

2 take away 1 makes ☐

☐ left

4 take away 1 makes ☐

☐ left

49

2 fewer than

Count how many.   ✔ 2 fewer.

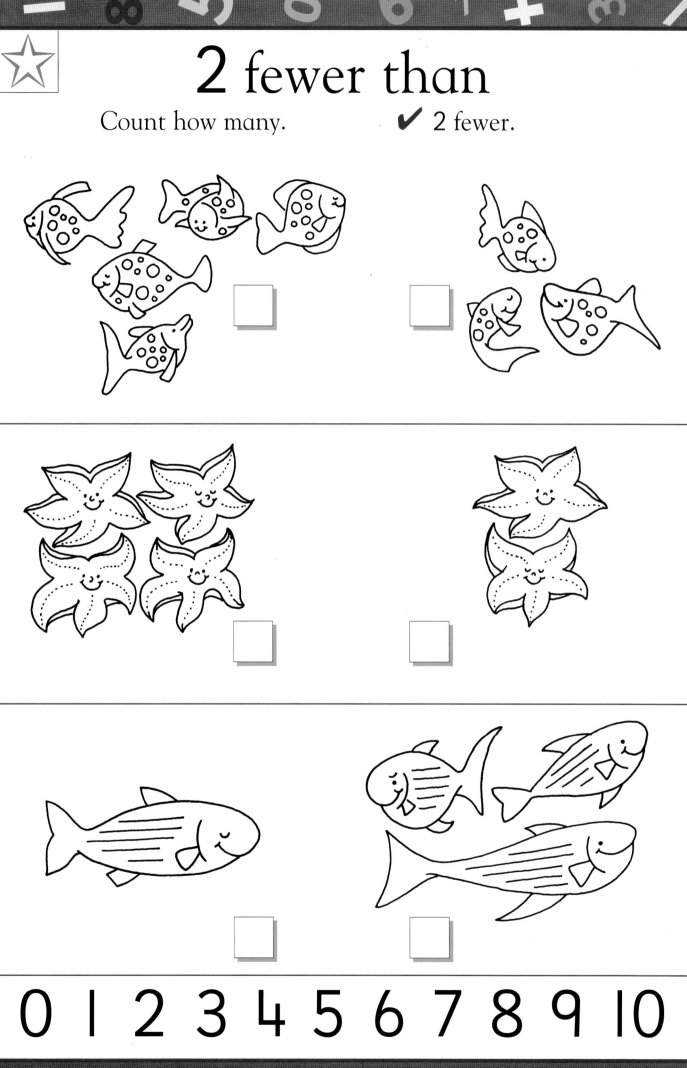

0 1 2 3 4 5 6 7 8 9 10

Take 2 away

✗ 2 out.   Count how many are left.

4 take away 2 makes ☐

5 take away 2 makes ☐

6 take away 2 makes ☐

0 1 2 3 4 5 6 7 8 9 10

3 fewer than

Count how many apples.

Draw 3 fewer apples on this tree.

Count how many apples.

Draw 3 fewer apples on this tree.

Count how many apples.

0 1 2 3 4 5 6 7 8 9 10

Take **3** away

✗ 3 out. Count how many are left.

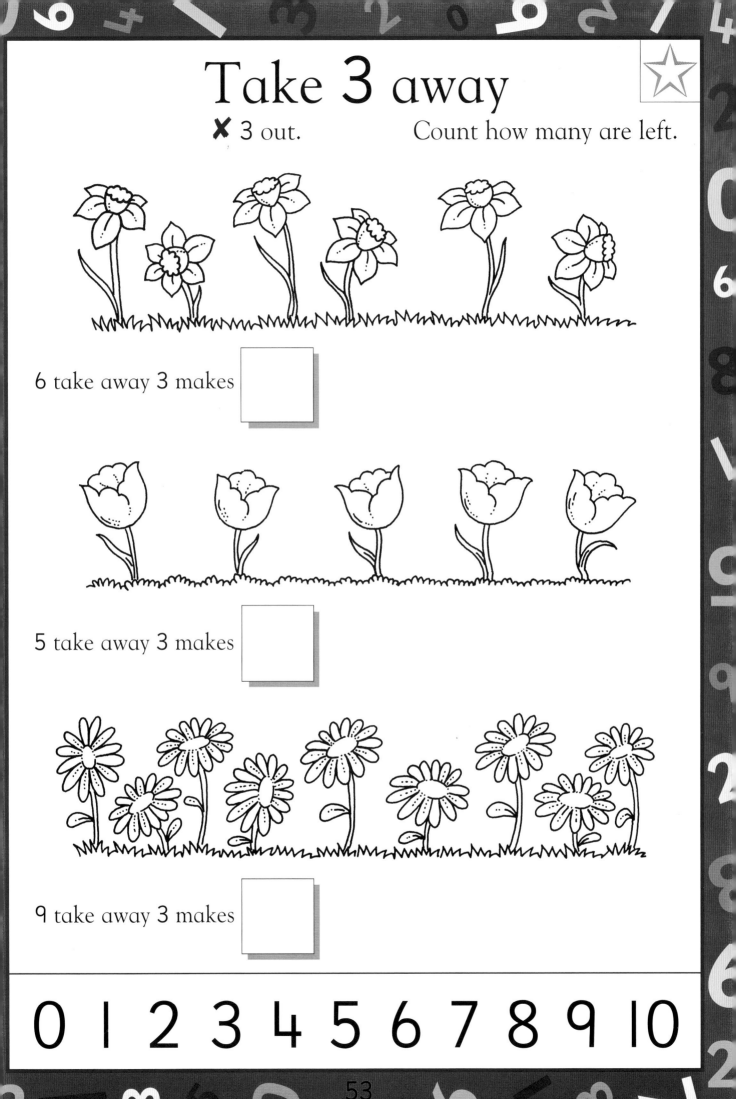

6 take away 3 makes

5 take away 3 makes

9 take away 3 makes

0 1 2 3 4 5 6 7 8 9 10

4 fewer than

Count how many. ✔ 4 fewer.

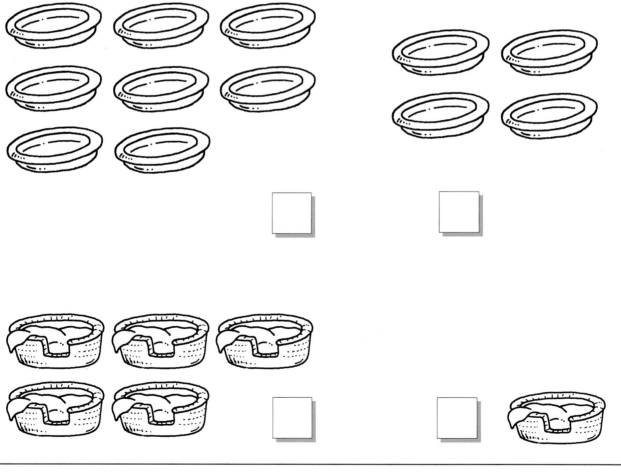

Take 4 away

✘ 4 out.   Count how many are left.

8 take away 4 makes [ ]

5 take away 4 makes [ ]

4 take away 4 makes [ ]

0 1 2 3 4 5 6 7 8 9 10

5 fewer than

Count how many. ✔ 5 fewer.

0 1 2 3 4 5 6 7 8 9 10

Take 5 away

✗ 5 out. Count how many are left.

9 take away 5 makes ☐

7 take away 5 makes ☐

5 take away 5 makes ☐

0 1 2 3 4 5 6 7 8 9 10

How many are left?

✗ 1 out. **✗** 2 out.

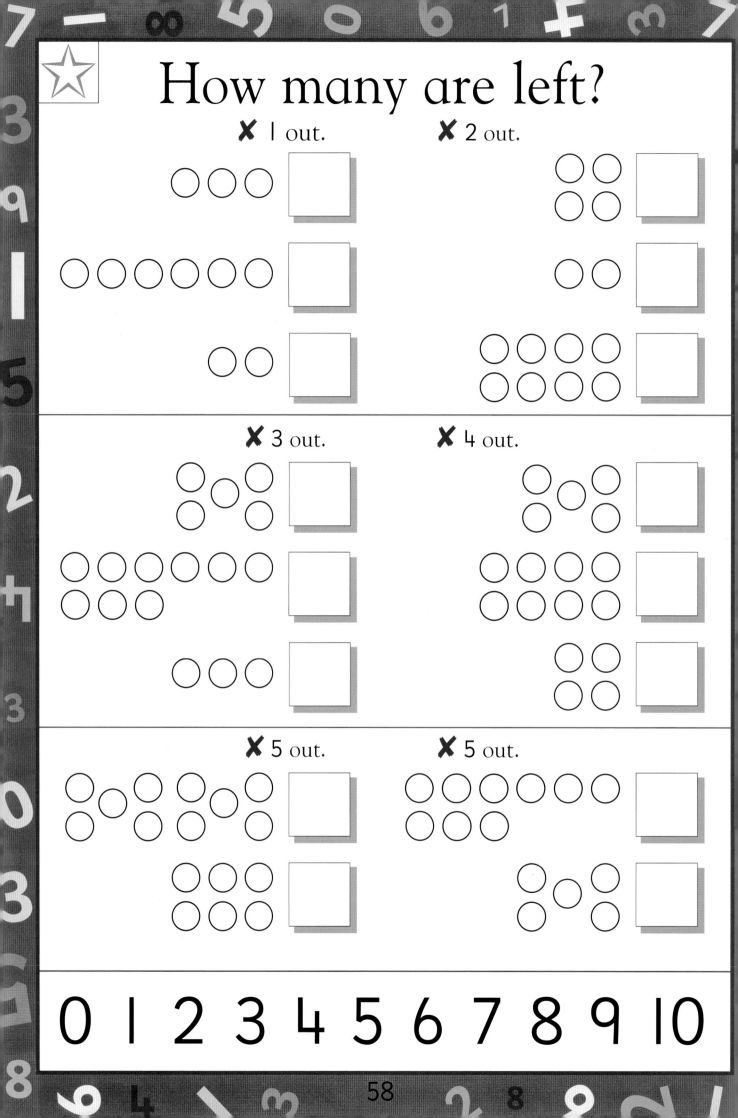

✗ 3 out. **✗** 4 out.

✗ 5 out. **✗** 5 out.

0 1 2 3 4 5 6 7 8 9 10

Take away

3 take away 2 makes ☐

4 take away 1 makes ☐

6 take away 2 makes ☐

5 take away 3 makes ☐

10 take away 1 makes ☐

7 take away 5 makes ☐

3 take away 3 makes ☐

8 take away 2 makes ☐

9 take away 1 makes ☐

6 take away 5 makes ☐

4 take away 4 makes ☐

7 take away 2 makes ☐

8 take away 4 makes ☐

10 take away 2 makes ☐

0 1 2 3 4 5 6 7 8 9 10

Special symbols

+ means **and**.   = means **equals**.

Count how many.

○○
○ and ○○ equals [ ]

3 and 2 equals [ ]

3 + 2 = [ ]

○○ and ○ equals [ ]

2 and 1 equals [ ]

2 + 1 = [ ]

○○
○○ and ○○ equals [ ]

4 and 2 equals [ ]

4 + 2 = [ ]

0 1 2 3 4 5 6 7 8 9 10

Special symbols

— means **take away** or **subtract**.　　= means **equals**.

Count how many.

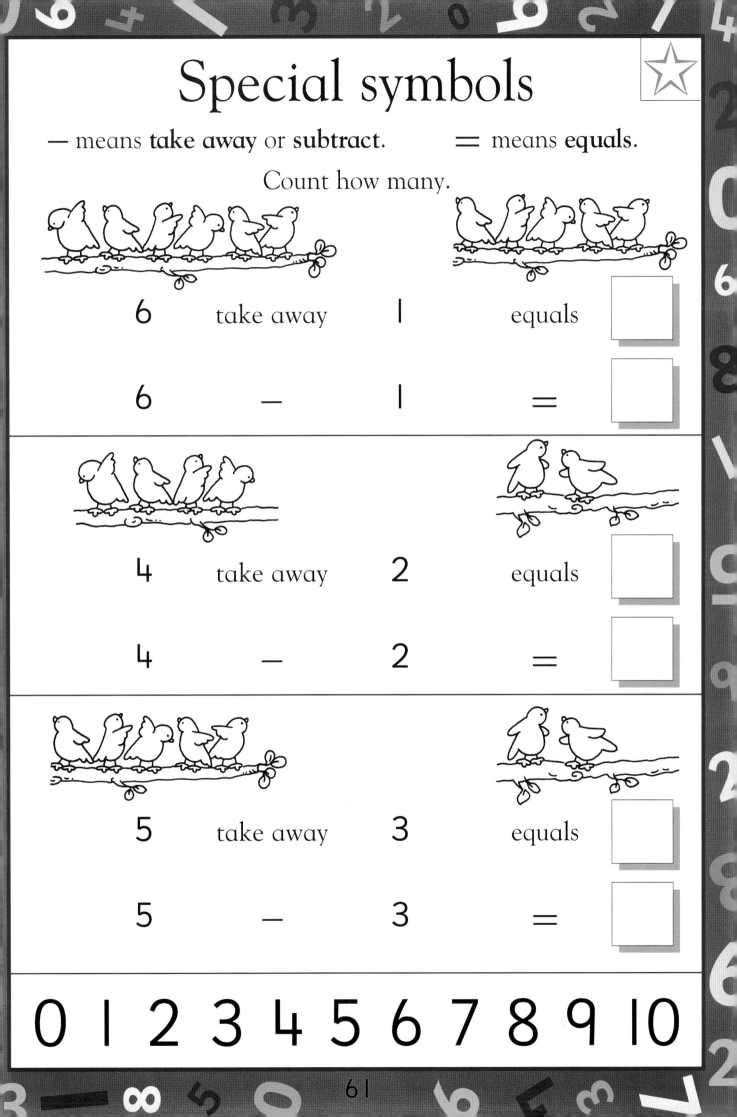

6　　take away　　1　　equals

6　　　—　　　1　　　=

4　　take away　　2　　equals

4　　　—　　　2　　　=

5　　take away　　3　　equals

5　　　—　　　3　　　=

0 1 2 3 4 5 6 7 8 9 10

Now you can do these

4 + 2 = ☐   6 – 1 = ☐

2 + 2 = ☐   5 – 3 = ☐

3 + 3 = ☐   4 – 4 = ☐

7 + 1 = ☐   10 – 2 = ☐

6 – 4 = ☐   9 – 3 = ☐

5 + 5 = ☐   6 + 3 = ☐

7 – 2 = ☐   5 + 4 = ☐

2 + 5 = ☐   1 – 1 = ☐

Write the symbol.

3 ☐ 1 = 4   3 ☐ 2 = 1

2 ☐ 2 = 4   4 ☐ 1 = 3

0 1 2 3 4 5 6 7 8 9 10

More than

Look. ✔ the necklace with more beads.

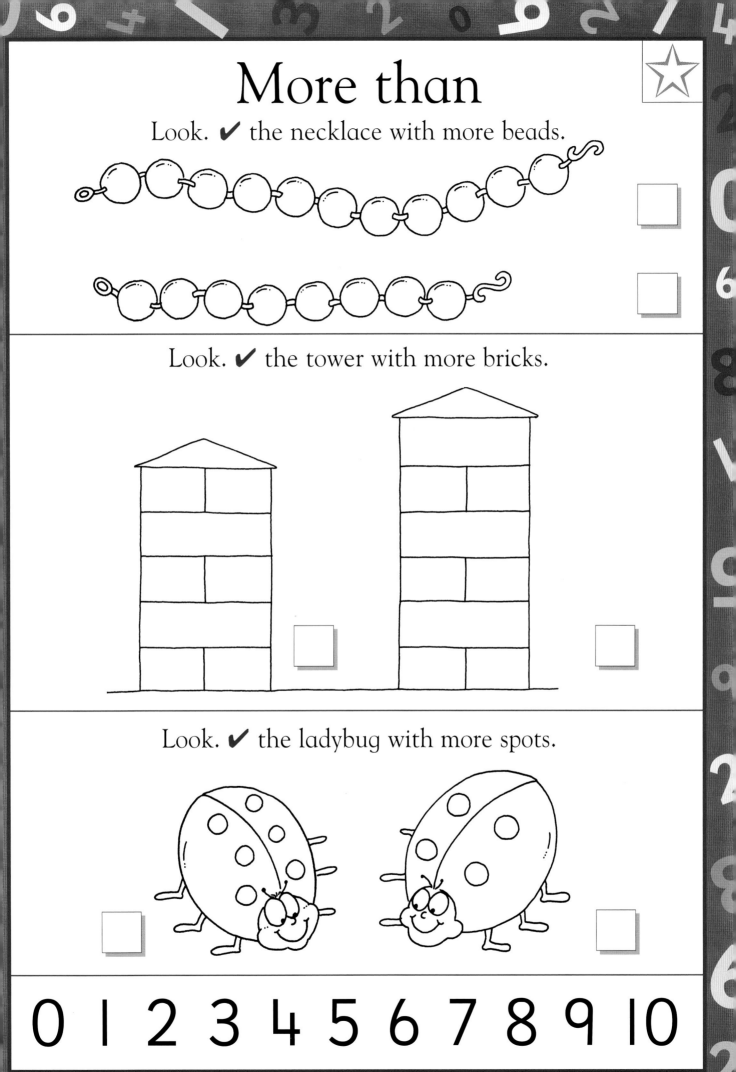

Look. ✔ the tower with more bricks.

Look. ✔ the ladybug with more spots.

0 1 2 3 4 5 6 7 8 9 10

Draw the shape

Count how many circles.

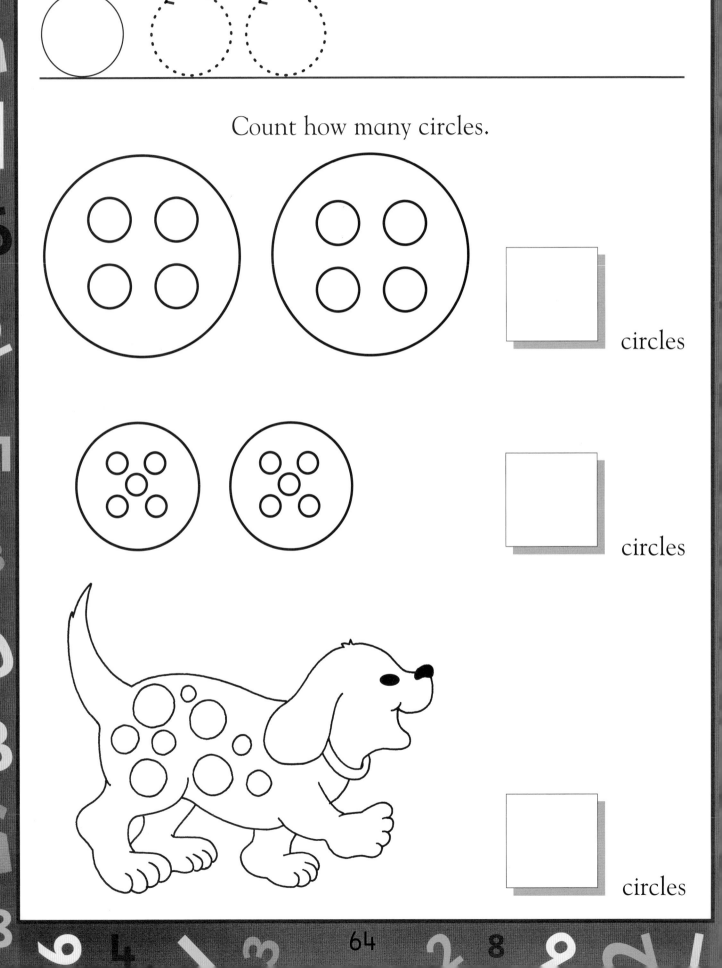

circles

circles

circles

Write the word

blue blue

Color the circles blue.

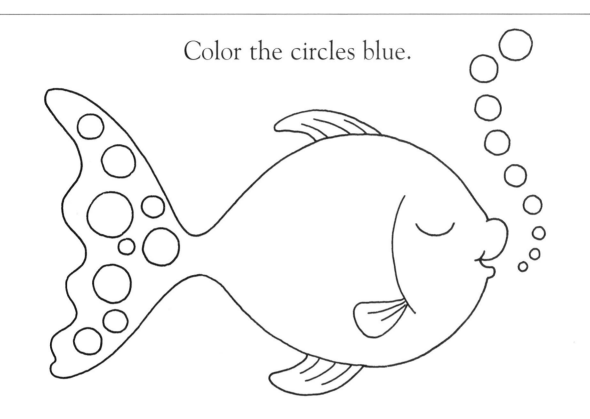

Draw the wheels on the cars.

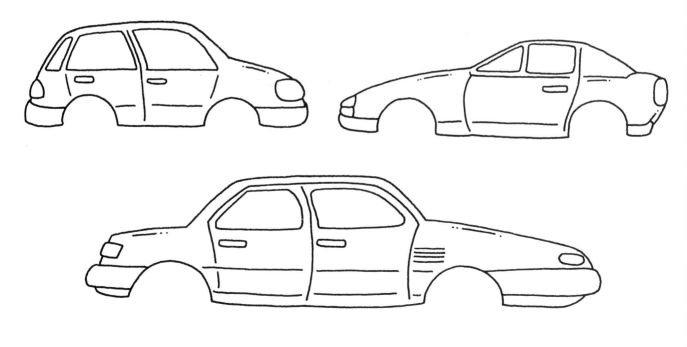

Draw the shape

Count how many squares.

squares

squares

squares

Write the word

green green

Color the squares green.

Draw a square house with
a door and 4 square windows.

Draw the shape

Count how many triangles.

triangles

triangles

triangles

Write the word

red red

Color the triangles red.

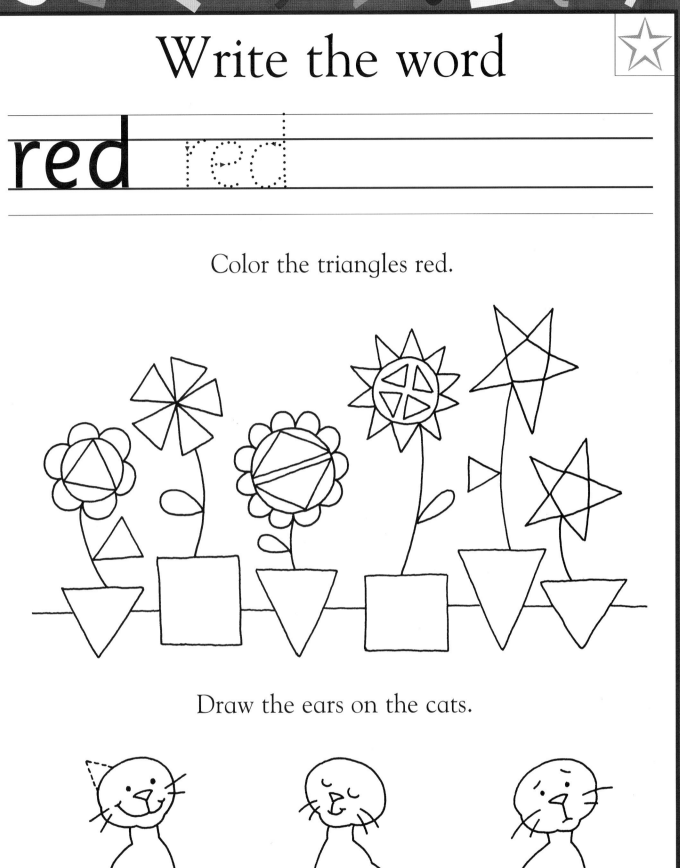

Draw the ears on the cats.

Draw the shape

Count how many rectangles.

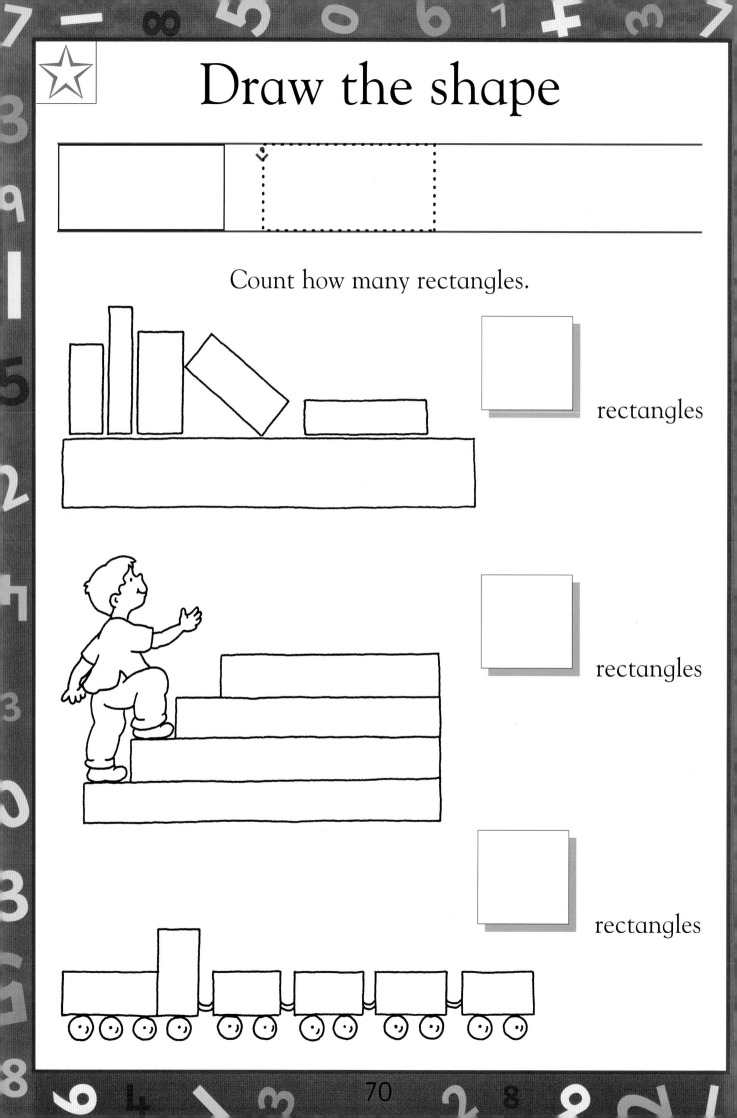

rectangles

rectangles

rectangles

Write the word

yellow yellow

Color the rectangles yellow.

Draw a wall for Humpty using rectangles.

Match the shapes

Draw blue lines.

Draw green lines.

Draw red lines.

Draw yellow lines.

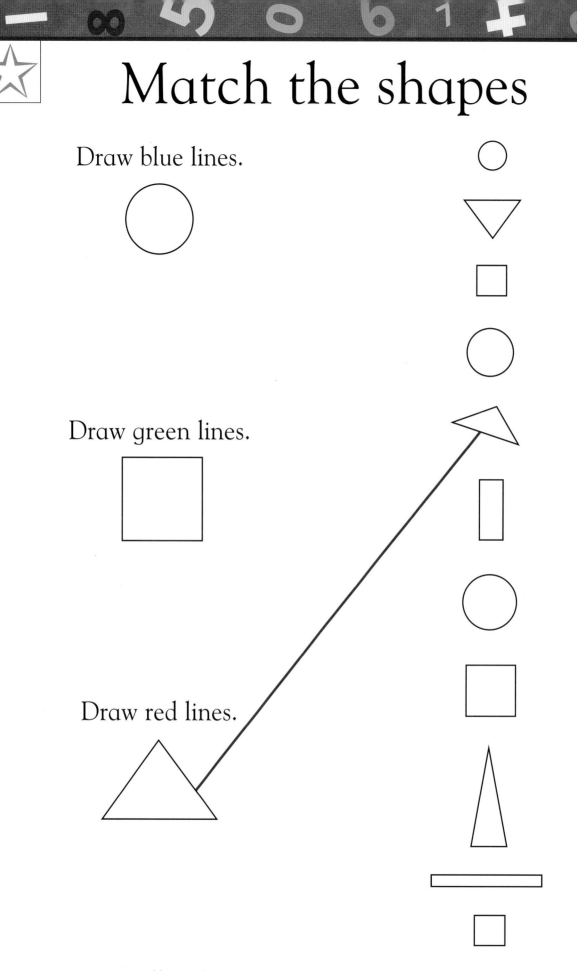

Color the pattern

○ circles – blue   △ triangles – red

▢ squares – green   ▭ rectangles – yellow

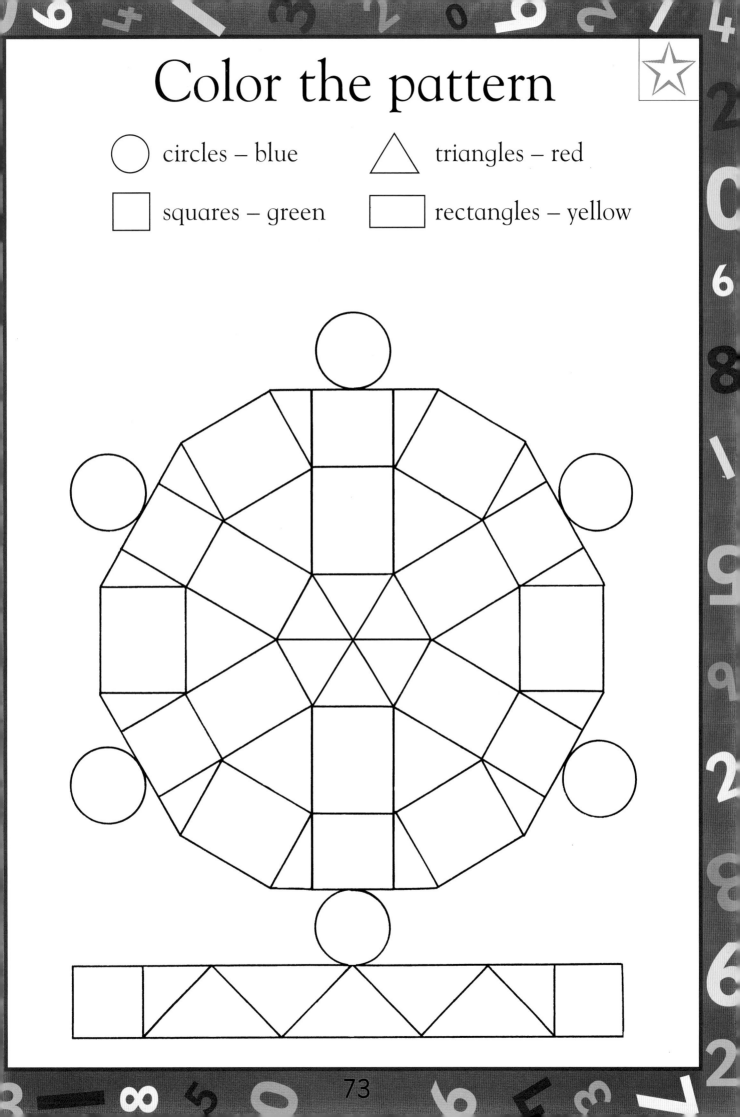

Big, bigger, biggest

★

A big shell

Draw a bigger shell.

A big fish

Draw a bigger fish.

Ring the biggest duck.

Ring the biggest frog.

Small, smaller, smallest

Small cup cake

Draw a smaller cup cake.

Small cup

Draw a smaller cup.

✔ the smallest.

Long, longer, longest

A long worm

Draw a longer worm.

A long necklace

Draw a longer necklace.

✔ the longest.

Short, shorter, shortest

A short tail

Draw a shorter tail.

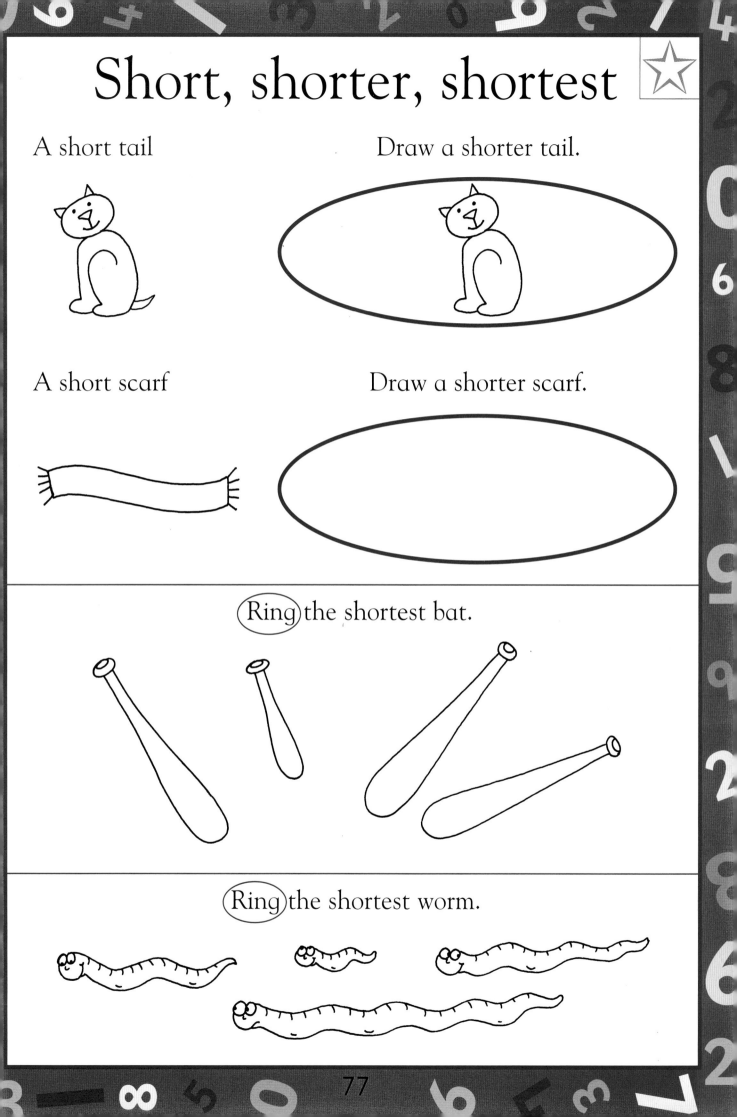

A short scarf

Draw a shorter scarf.

Ring the shortest bat.

Ring the shortest worm.

Tall, taller, tallest

A tall bottle

Draw a taller bottle.

A tall flower

Draw a taller flower.

✔ the tallest.

Short, shorter, shortest

A short tree

Draw a shorter tree.

A short string

Draw a shorter string.

✔ the shortest.

Thick, thicker, thickest

A thick tree trunk

Draw a thicker tree trunk.

A thick candle

Draw a thicker candle.

Ring the thickest.

Thin, thinner, thinnest

A thin house

Draw a thinner house.

A thin balloon

Draw a thinner balloon.

Ring the thinnest.

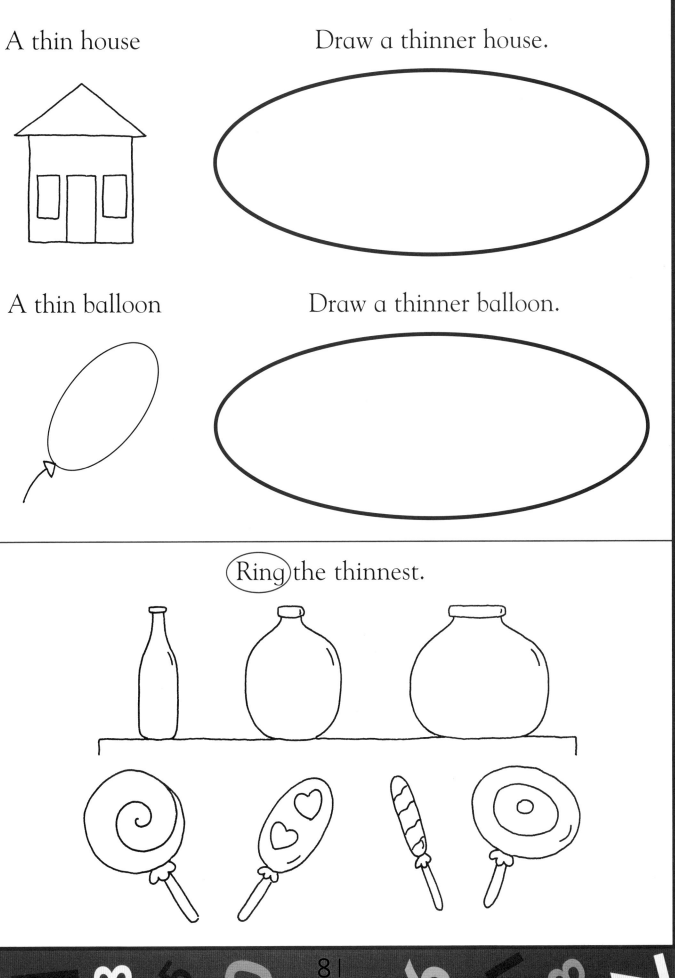

Color

Color the biggest one red.

Color the tallest one green.

Color the longest one blue.

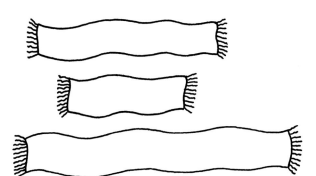

Color the thinnest one yellow.

Draw and color

Draw a bigger circle.   Color it blue.

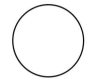

Draw a longer rectangle.   Color it green.

Draw a bigger triangle.   Color it red.

Draw a thicker rectangle.   Color it yellow.

Draw a bigger square.   Color it blue.

In front

✔ if the book is in front.

Draw a cat in front of the house.

Behind

✔ if the mouse is behind.

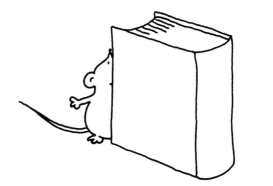

Inside

✔ if something is inside.

Draw a circle inside the square.

Outside

✔ if something is outside.

Draw 2 candies outside the jar.

Between

Draw a ball between

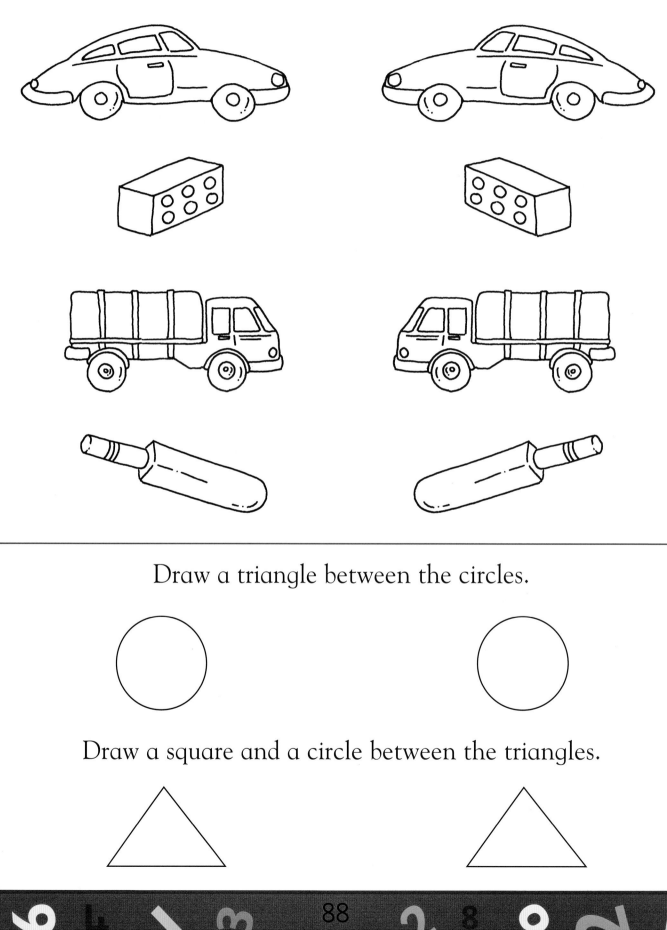

Draw a triangle between the circles.

Draw a square and a circle between the triangles.

Beside

Draw a ball beside the teddy bear.

Draw a cup beside the teddy bear.

Draw a book beside the teddy bear.

Draw a circle beside the square.

Above, on, and below

Draw 2 birds above the boat.

Draw 3 fish below the boat.

Draw 2 ducks on the water.

Above, on, and below

How many things are on the ground?

	on

How many are above the ground?

	above

How many are below the ground?

	below

Finish the picture

Draw the sun above the castle.

Draw a door between the square windows.

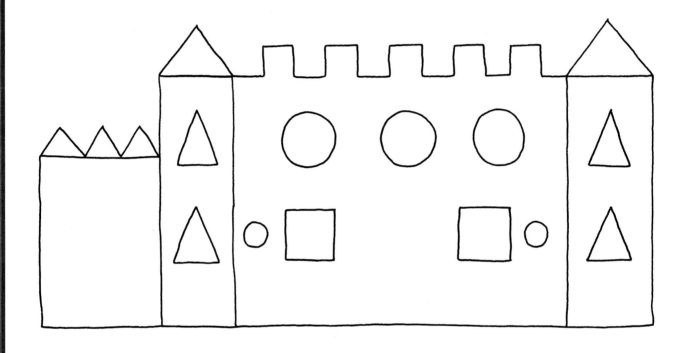

How many circles?

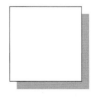

How many squares?

How many rectangles?

How many triangles?

Finish the picture

Draw a frog beside the fairy.

Draw a wand in the fairy's hand.

Draw some stars above the fairy.

Draw some flowers below the fairy.

☆ What shapes can you see?

Different

Ring the sock that is different.

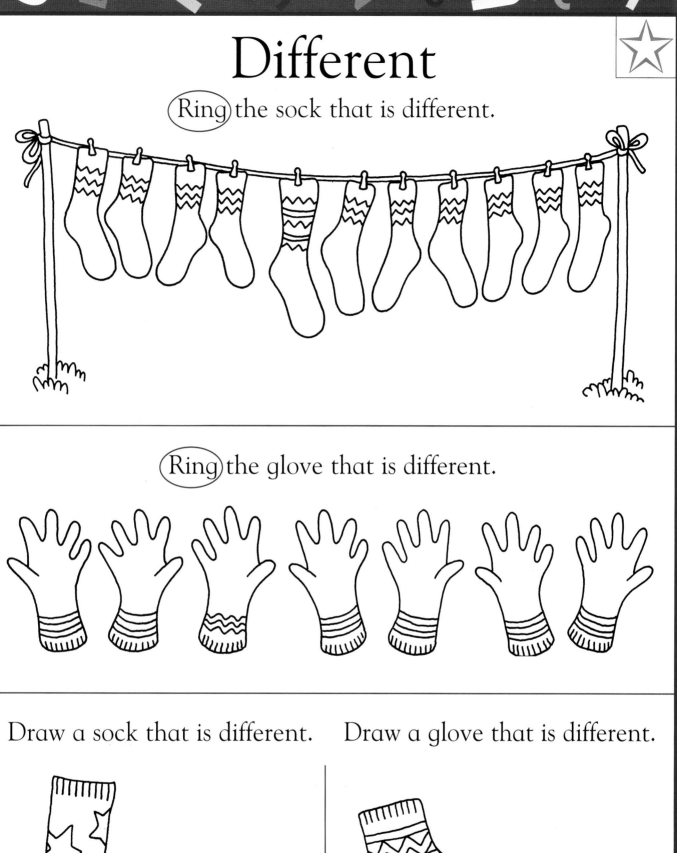

Ring the glove that is different.

Draw a sock that is different.   Draw a glove that is different.

Different

Ring the flag that is different.

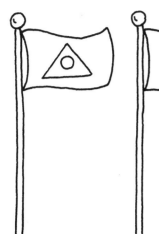

Draw the flag that is different.

Draw a flag that is not different.

Different numbers

Count how many spots are on the big ladybug.

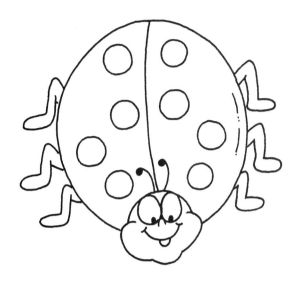

Draw a ⟨ring⟩ around the ladybug with
a different number of spots.

Draw a ⟨ring⟩ around the ladybug with
a different number of spots.

Different numbers

Draw a different number of shapes on the umbrellas.

The same

Match the animals.

Draw and color **2** animals that are the same.

The same

Draw lines to match the shoes that are the same. Make pairs.

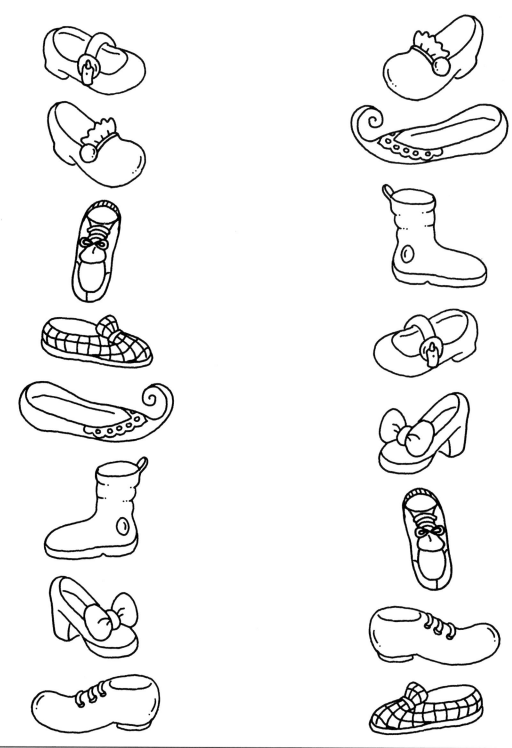

Draw a pair of shoes for yourself.

The same

Find the big triangles △. Color them red.
Find the small circles ○. Color them blue.

Count how many
red triangles.

Count how many
blue circles.

The same

Draw lines to match the monsters.

The same

Draw the other half to match.

Sorting sets

Draw a line to the right set.

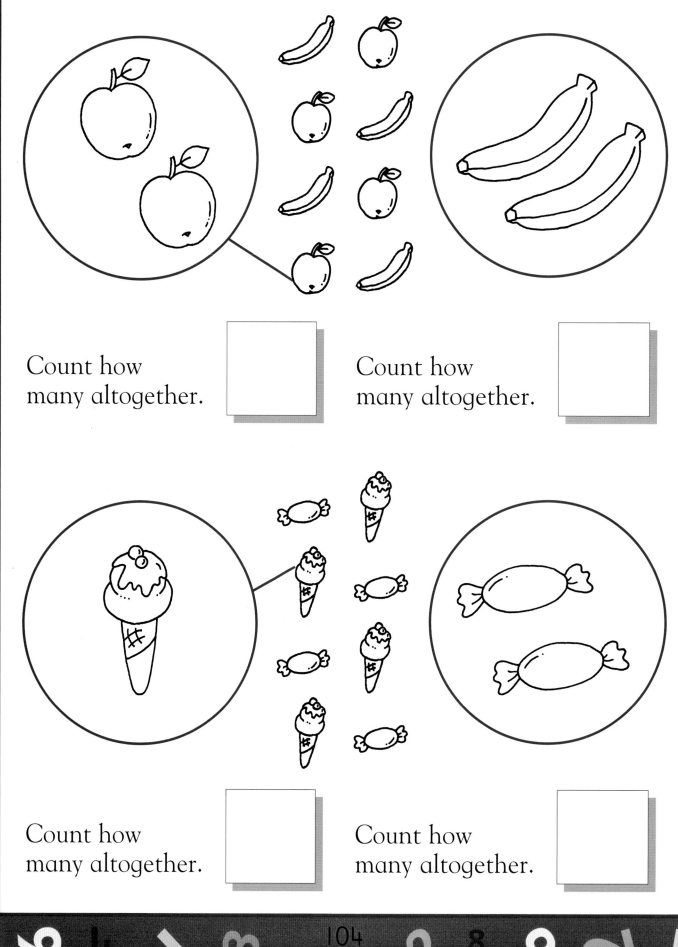

Count how
many altogether.

Count how
many altogether.

Count how
many altogether.

Count how
many altogether.

Adding to sets

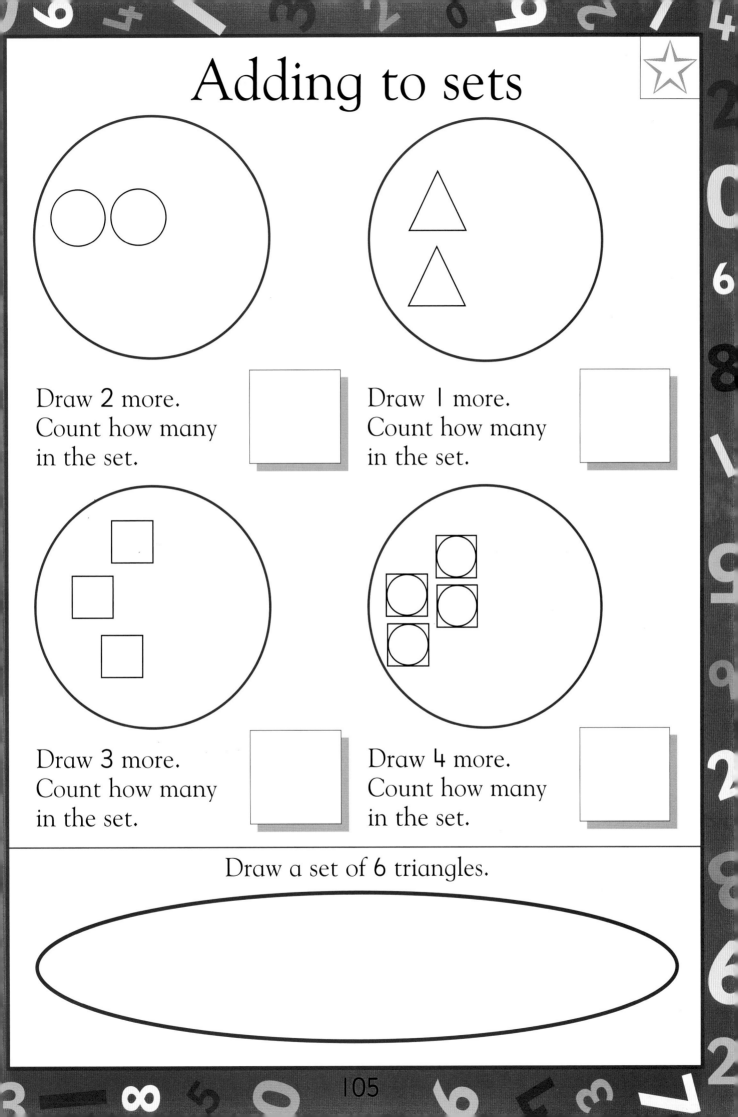

Draw **2** more.
Count how many
in the set.

Draw **1** more.
Count how many
in the set.

Draw **3** more.
Count how many
in the set.

Draw **4** more.
Count how many
in the set.

Draw a set of **6** triangles.

Sorting the toys

Look at the toys in the circles.
Match the other toys to the right circle.

Sorting the trees

Count how many apples are on each tree.

How many trees have...

3 apples?	

4 apples?	

5 apples?	

Draw 1 more tree for each set.

Now how many trees have...

3 apples?	

4 apples?	

5 apples?	

Sorting the animals

Look at the animals. Count how many legs they have.
Match them to the right part of the boat.

2 legs

0 legs

4 legs

6 legs

Sorting the animals

Count how many legs.
Ring the animals with the number of legs shown in the box.

a lion   a bird   a sheep   a fish   4 legs

a fish   a duck   a ladybug   a cat   6 legs

a giraffe   a bird   a lion   a sheep   2 legs

an elephant   a fish   a bird   a mouse   0 legs

Sorting the fish

Match the fish to the fishermen's numbers.

Sorting the fish

Match the fish to the fishermen's hats.

Count how many fish.

Identifying the patterns

Continue each pattern.

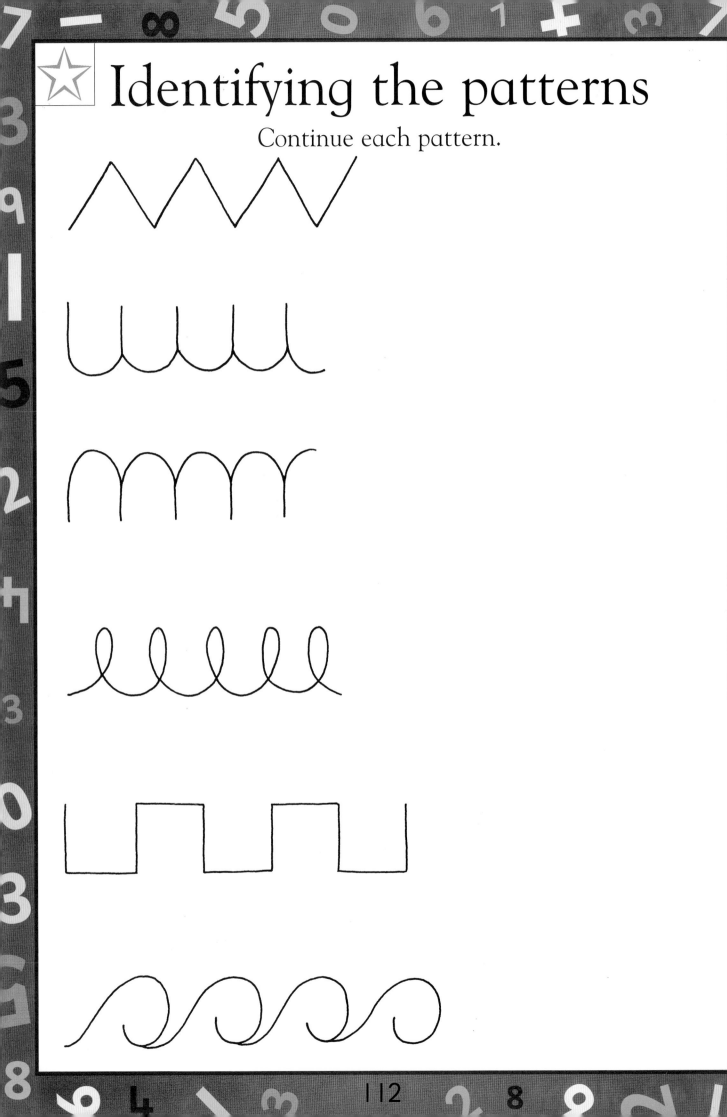

Identifying the patterns

Complete each pattern.

Draw your own patterns.

Identifying the patterns

Continue each pattern.

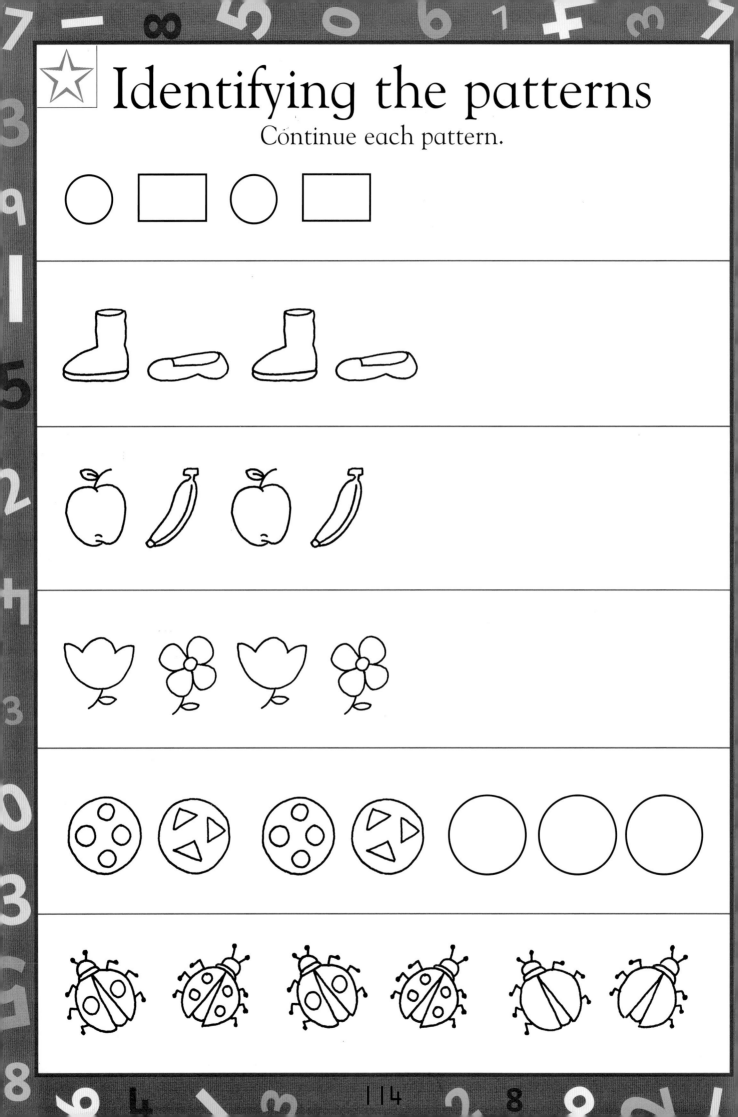

Identifying the patterns

Continue each pattern.

| 1 | 2 | 1 | 2 | | | | |

| 6 | 7 | 8 | 6 | 7 | 8 | | | |

115

In the right order

✔ before.

✔ after.

Write 1st, 2nd, and 3rd in the boxes.

In the right order

Talk about the pictures.
Write 1st, 2nd, and 3rd in the boxes.

Talk about the pictures.
Write 1st, 2nd, and 3rd in the boxes.

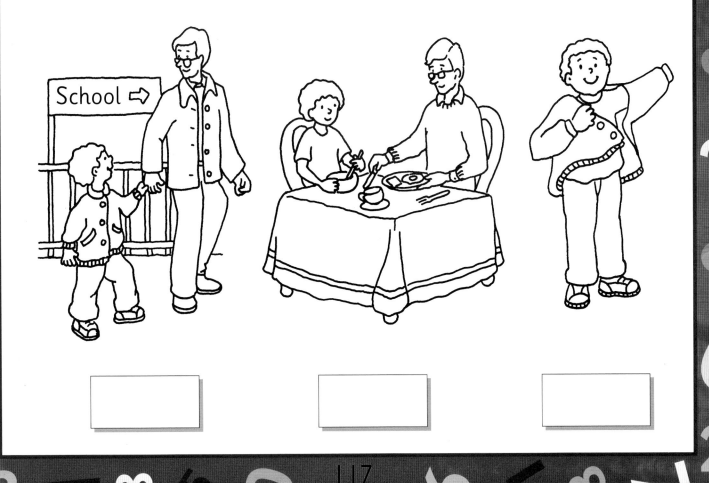

Identifying patterns

Finish the pattern.

Finish the pattern.

Finish the pattern.

Draw the missing caterpillar.

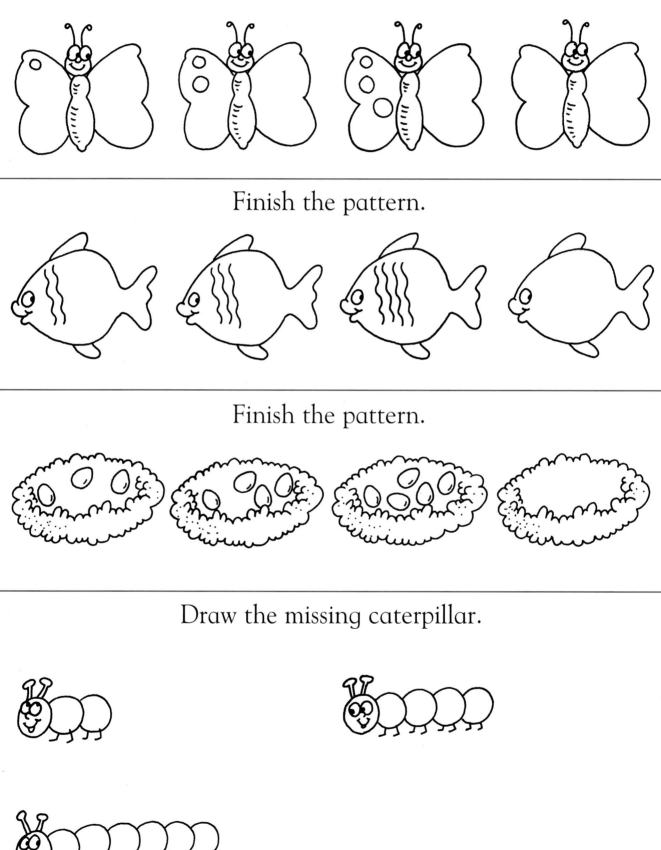

The missing numbers

Write the missing numbers.

Write the missing numbers.

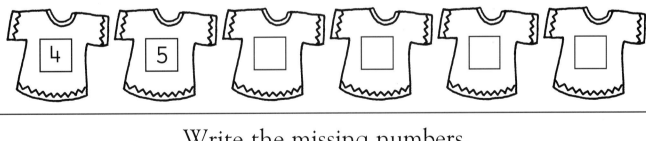

Write the missing numbers.

Mary sorted her snails

Sort the snails. Draw a line to connect each snail to the correct circle.

Count how many of each type there are.

Mary grew some flowers

Draw a (ring) around the different flower.

Draw a flower that is the same.

The maze

Follow the pattern to find your way out.

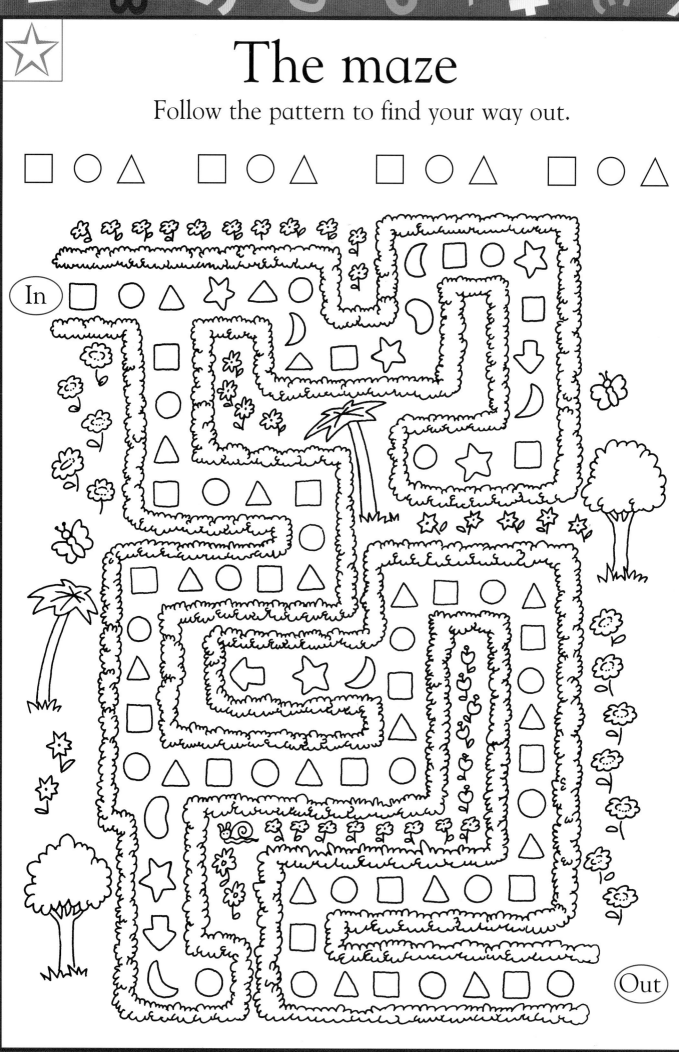

Dot-to-dot

Connect the dots.

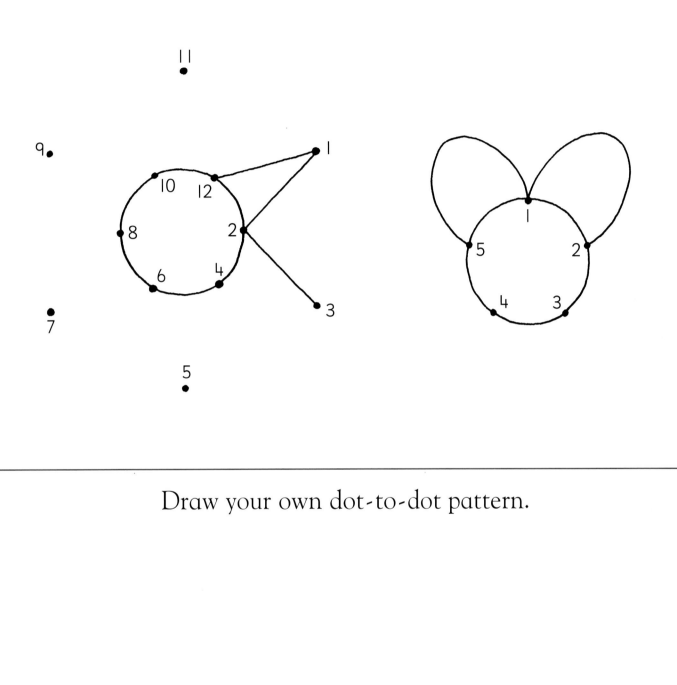

Draw your own dot-to-dot pattern.

Different

Ring the animal that is different.

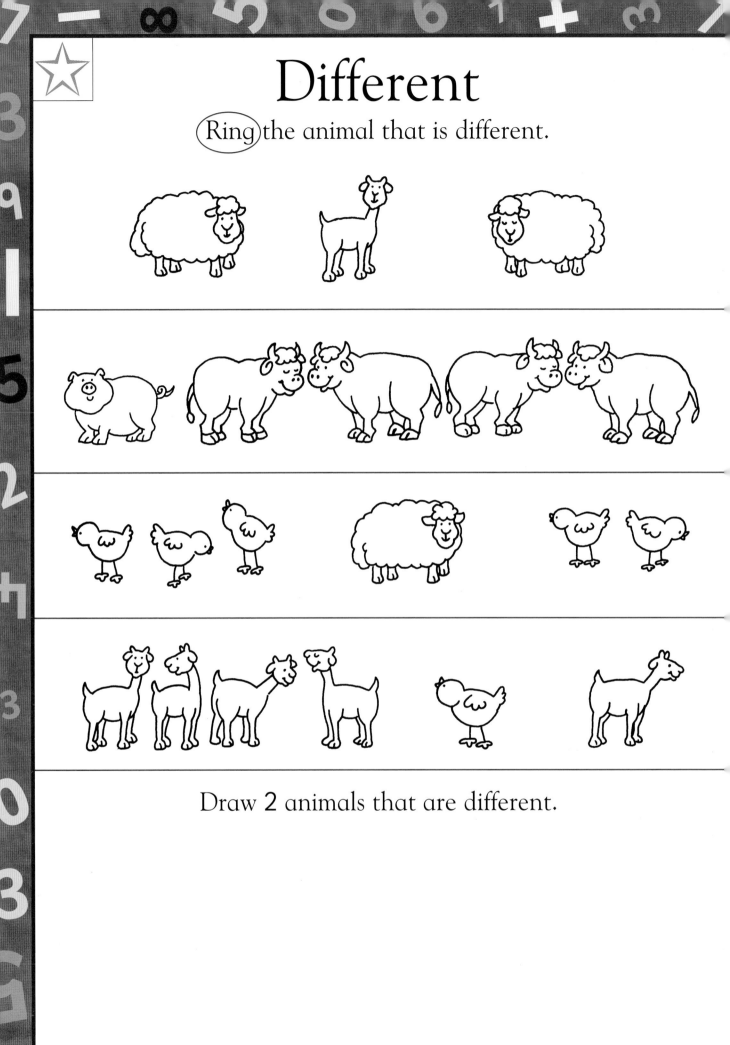

Draw **2** animals that are different.

Notes for parents (Pages 2–32)

This book is designed to help you and your child explore the fascinating world of numbers in a fun and enjoyable way. Most children learn to count from a very early age, and this book will help them learn important skills and mathematical concepts.

Content
By working through this section your child will learn:
- Names of the numbers 1–10 and 11–20.
- Sequence, or order, of the numbers.
- Number values. Understanding the quantity that each number represents and that, for example, 5 is always 5. It may be 5 big buses in a row or 5 small peas in a circle, but it is still 5!
- That when counting, the last number names the set. Many children count the quantity accurately 1, 2, 3, 4, but in response to "how many?" often say the wrong number.
- How to recognize written numbers.
- How to write numbers.
- How to recognize a number when it is written in words, and how to write it.

How to help your child
A child learns through hands-on experiences—it will be helpful if your child has had a range of practical counting experiences before attempting the activities in the section.

This book should be enjoyable for both you and your child—a shared time together. Make sure that your child is alert and not too tired. Keep the time spent appropriate to the age of the child and his or her level of concentration. Build your child's confidence by praise and encouragement. Celebrate his or her success.

The activities are similar throughout the book but are more difficult for higher numbers. Make sure your child is capable of coping with numbers beyond 10 before attempting pages 26–32.

Encourage your child to color in the illustrations. This develops pencil control, increases eye-hand coordination, and builds concentration.

Make sure there is a range of colored pencils or felt-tip pens available. Crayons are usually too thick for such activities.

For writing and drawing, your child will need a sharp, soft pencil. If the pencil is too hard, he or she will have difficulty seeing his or her work, and this will lead to frustration. Encourage your child to hold the pencil lightly between the thumb and forefinger, with the middle finger providing support. A lump of modeling clay molded to a triangular shape around the pencil helps with grip, one digit on each of the sides. Make sure the child doesn't hold it too near the point, as this will inhibit the flow in writing and drawing.

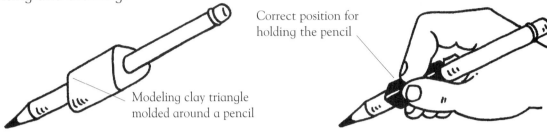

Correct position for holding the pencil

Modeling clay triangle molded around a pencil

When children are writing numbers and letters, they should always start from the top. Dots are provided to help your child practice writing numbers and words, and there is a dot to show your child where to begin when writing on his or her own.

To help your child form shapes of numbers and letters before using a pencil, encourage him or her to practice in sand or flour. Together with your child you can make the shapes out of any malleable material. Your child can then trace the letter or number shape with a finger.

Talk about the activities on each page and make sure your child understands what to do. Talk about the pictures. Numbers 1–10 are based on familiar nursery rhymes and fairy tales, so talk about the characters and say the rhymes together. This will give your child a context for the activities.

Remember this book is meant to be fun as well as educational, so stop before your child loses concentration or becomes restless. This will ensure that he or she will want to come back for more!

How to use the book

There are several short tasks on each page. For numbers 1–10 there are two pages relating to each number.

It is important to consolidate what a child has learned, so review pages are included after number 5 and number 10.

There are two numbers on each page for numbers beyond 10 with a fun dot-to-dot at the end!

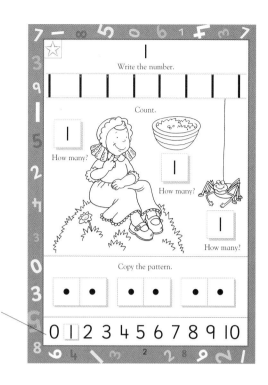

Number line

Write the number

Trace the dots and then practice writing the number. Talk to your child about the number, how it looks, the shape of it, and where he or she has seen it before—such as, in your address.

Count how many

When counting, encourage your child to put a finger on each object as he or she counts it, and then write the number in the box. Frequently, objects are arranged in different ways to introduce the idea that quantities can be presented in various ways but they still make the same number. It will also help your child to recognize that 8, for example, can be made up of two fours, a four and two twos, and so on. Talk about this with your child. Before using the pages, it is a good idea to explore this in a practical, fun way by arranging candies, beans, or apples in a variety of ways.

Copy the pattern

The numbers are displayed as dominoes. This is one way of helping your child to recognize quantities at a glance.

Number line

This is on each page to familiarize your child with number sequences. Encourage your child to fill in the missing number on each page, to point to and say the numbers out loud, and to write the numbers in the boxes.

Although the book begins at number 1, the number line includes 0. The concept of zero is difficult to grasp at the early stages of counting, and is more relevant when subtraction is introduced. Zero has been included here because children may come across it in other contexts such as rhymes that involve counting back 3, 2, 1, 0, take-off!

Write the word

Encourage your child to follow the dots, starting at the top and writing each letter in a continuous movement. Dots are provided for children to write the letters on their own.

Other activities on the page will include drawing, matching, and putting rings around numbers. These vary for each number.

Page-by-page notes

Page 2 – Number 1

The first two pages feature the rhyme *Little Miss Muffet*. Say the rhyme and talk about how many girls, spiders, and bowls there are. Recall what other rhymes feature the number 1—*Little Jack Horner*, for example. Get your child to write the number making sure he or she starts at the top and keeps within the guidelines.

Page 3 – Write the word

Talk about the bowls. Are they like your bowls? Draw the spoons. Who will eat from the bowls, what sort of spoon will he or she use, is it big or small? Match by drawing a line from the number 1 to the groups that have only one item. Your child doesn't have to know how many are in the other groups, only that they have more than one item. Encourage your child to color both pages.

Page 4 – Number 2

Have your child write the number. Talk about the shape. What does it remind your child of? A swan, perhaps? When your child is writing the number, talk about the movements of the pencil—up, over the top, down and along. Repeat these when he or she is writing on his or her own without the dots. Talk about things that go in pairs—socks and shoes, for example.

Page 5 – Write the word

Make sure your child starts at the top. Drawing rabbits and fish may be difficult for very young children, so praise their attempts. Have your child match the groups with two items to the number 2 by drawing a line.

Page 6 – Number 3

Have your child write the number. Talk about its shape and about seeing the number in other contexts. Describe the movement of the pencil—up, over, halfway around, and halfway around again. This number is based on the story of *Goldilocks and the Three Bears*. Does your child know any other stories or rhymes that have the number 3 in them—*Three Billy Goats Gruff, Three Blind Mice*? Encourage your child to point to each object as it is counted.

Page 7 – Write the word

Encourage your child to notice that "h" is a tall letter. Have your child draw a ring round each set of three. The word "sets" describes, in mathematical terms, a group, and it is a word with which your child should become familiar. To reinforce drawing a ring, he or she should identify the number of items in each set by ringing the number.

Page 8 – Number 4

Have your child write the number. Talk about how to move the pencil starting at the top, straight down, then to the right, and then in a straight line from top to bottom. Talk about the number in context. *Little Bo Peep* is the nursery rhyme, where her sheep number four. The sets of four are arranged in different ways as explained in the earlier notes. When counting, ensure that your child points to each object, and that the last number counted names the set.

Page 9

Matching and drawing activities.

Page 10 – Number 5

Have your child write the number. Make sure your child starts at the dot and comes down and around (a big fat tummy!) and then puts the hat on, starting at the dot, and going from left to right. *One two three four five, Once I caught a fish alive* is the nursery rhyme. Talk about other fives: fingers or toes, for example. Again the objects are arranged in different ways.

Page 11

A counting activity and drawing his or her own set of five.

Page 12 – Review

Review of numbers 1–5. Writing all five numbers, counting, and recording.

Page 13 – Review

Matching the written word to the number and matching the numbers to the quantities.

Page 14 – Number 6

Have your child write the number—starting at the top, then down and all the way around. It is important that your child begins to learn how to write the numbers correctly. It is difficult to unlearn mistakes. The cookies are arranged in several different ways. The dominoes show six in the traditional formation of two threes, and as five and one.

Page 15

Matching and drawing activities.

Page 16 – Number 7

Get your child to write the number 7, making sure he or she begins on the dot, draws from left to right, then down to the left. *Mary Mary Quite Contrary* is the nursery rhyme and her flowers are arranged in a variety of ways. The dominoes show seven as five and two and as four and three. These patterns will help your child become familiar with what makes seven, which will help later on when he or she is adding.

Page 17

The activities include counting and drawing rings around the numbers to match the sets.

Page 18 – Number 8

Writing the number 8 can be quite difficult for young children, but it is important that they write without taking their pencil off the paper.
The nursery rhyme is *Wee Willie Winkie*.

Page 19

These activities introduce counting forward and counting backward as well as the numbers on a clock face.

Page 20 – Number 9

Your child should write the number without taking the pencil off the paper. This is difficult as children frequently draw the circle and add the stick. The rhyme is *Twinkle Twinkle Little Star*.

Page 21

These activities include drawing and matching.

Page 22 – Number 10

Your child should write the number, making sure to start both digits at the top. The theme is *Ten Green Bottles*.

Page 23

The activities are counting and ringing the number that matches the set.

Page 24 – Review

This is a review of numbers 6–10. Your child has to match the written word to the number, and count and record numbers up to 10.

Page 25

A dot-to-dot, practicing the order of numbers 1–10.

Page 26 – Numbers 11 and 12

Make sure your child has had many practical experiences of counting and handling quantities greater than 10. The quantities are arranged in sets showing that, for example, 11 is 10 and 1, as well as a group of 11. The number line shows numbers 10–20. There is no theme to these later pages.

Page 27 – Numbers 13 and 14

The activities are counting the number in a set, and drawing sets. Your child will need to point carefully to each object in a set, and count and check as he or she is drawing sets.

Page 28 – Numbers 15 and 16

Your child has to ring the correct number in each set.

Page 29 – Numbers 17 and 18

Your child has to match the sets to the right number by drawing a line.

Page 30 – Numbers 19 and 20

The activity is counting the number in each set.

Page 31

This activity introduces the idea of counting forward. Your child has to complete the number sequence. Encourage your child to count from the number given and not go back to 1.

Page 32

A fun page of dot-to-dot, reviewing the order of numbers from 1–20.

Notes for parents (Pages 33–63)

This section of the book is designed for children who have the ability to count from zero to 20, with a good understanding of the order and value of numbers. If your child has these skills, he or she is probably ready to explore problem solving with numbers.

Content

By working through this section your child will discover the fun of adding numbers together and subtracting them. Your child will learn:

- the concept of *more than*, initially by looking and then by counting.
- the concept of adding numbers together.
- the language involved in the addition process.
- the symbols for addition.
- the concept of *less than*, *fewer than*, initially by looking and then by counting.
- the concept of subtraction.
- the language involved in the subtraction process.
- the symbols used in subtraction.
- the use of the symbols of both addition and subtraction to answer questions.

How to help your child

Your child should have had a range of practical addition and subtraction experiences before attempting the activities in this section. You can offer these hands-on experiences by adding and subtracting familiar objects. Your child may need buttons or similar small objects to work through the section. As he or she becomes confident and familiar with the activities, the drawn objects may be sufficient. But have something available just in case!

9

In most of the activities your child will be asked to fill in the missing numbers. Make sure he or she begins writing the number at the top. Your child can refer to the number line at any time.

There are similar activities throughout, but the section becomes more challenging as it progresses. The progression is gradual, beginning by adding one more, then two more, up to five. The same is true for subtracting: first taking one away, then two, up to five.

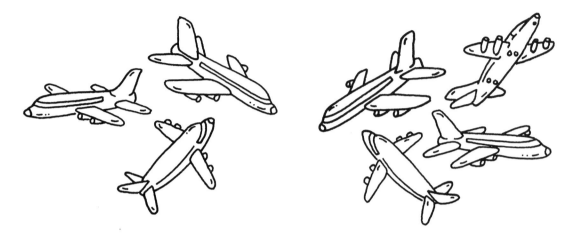

There are two review pages each for addition and subtraction.

The final three pages introduce math symbols and their position within problems.

Throughout the section, until the last three pages, words are used so your child may need help with reading.

Talk about the activities on each page and make sure your child understands what he or she should do.

Present the activities as practical problems when talking about them, as this will give your child a sense of using these number operations for a purpose. Without this practical application, your child will see activities as meaningless tasks with no relevance to his or her life. If this happens, your child will not be able to make full use of his or her understanding and skills later.

Vocabulary used in the section

more than	general statement to indicate that there is more in one set or group than in another
1 (2, 3, 4, 5) more than	to show how many more in a particular set
and 1 (2, 3, 4, 5) more	is the beginning of adding to a quantity
makes	is used instead of the symbol = For example, 3 and 1 more makes 4
fewer than	as a mathematical term this describes the difference between two numbers
1 (2, 3, 4, 5) fewer	this describes how many fewer in a set (The word *less* may also be used by the child)
take 1 (2, 3, 4, 5) away	this describes subtraction
left	this is used to tell what remains after subtraction
symbols	such as: +, − and =
+	means "and" or plus
−	means "take away" or subtract
=	means "makes" or equals

How to use the section

Be sure that your child has had many practical addition and subtraction experiences before starting each page.

Introduce your child to the vocabulary he or she will use in each activity.

Number line

There is a number line up to 10 at the bottom of each page. This will help your child recall what the numbers look like. The number line can also be used to encourage your child to count on.

Number line

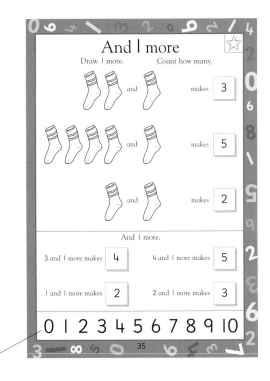

Counting forward and back

This can be introduced as a fun activity before starting the section. Create your own number line; it can go beyond 10. Encourage your child to count, using a hopping motion from number to number:

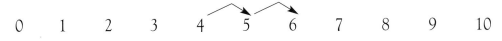

0   1   2   3   4   5   6   7   8   9   10

For example, for "4 and 2 more ..." put a finger on the number 4 and make the child do two jumps, first landing at 5 and then at 6, so that the answer is 6.

Subtraction can be done in the same way, by counting the number of jumps backward. Zero, or nothing, is introduced during the process of subtraction and is featured in the number line.

By progressing slowly through the section, exploring one number at a time, you can help your child become familiar with addition and subtraction, and help him or her with mental calculations.

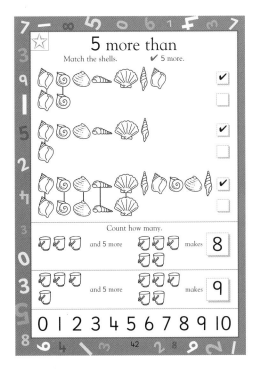

Page-by-page notes

Pages 34, 36, 38, 40, and 42 – Match

The rows have been arranged horizontally to help your child work out how many more there are in one set than another. Your child can match one object to another by drawing a line between the objects.

At the end of each row is a box. Your child should check the box at the end of the row that has *more* in it.

Count how many

Your child has to add on. For example, count how many hats 4 and 2 more hats make.

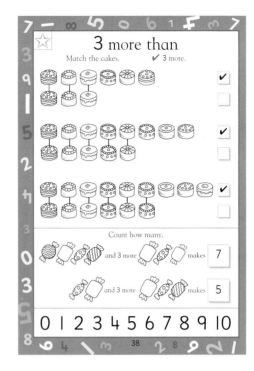

Encourage your child to count forward, starting at 4, on to 5, and then 6.

Use practical support such as buttons and fingers, until your child feels confident enough to manage without them.

It is a good idea to introduce counting on the number line. This will encourage your child to begin counting from the existing number instead of going back to number 1, which children frequently do.

Offer your child plenty of praise and encouragement.

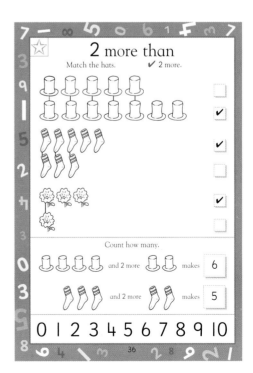

Pages 35, 37, 39, 41, 43 – And 1 more

Draw 1 (2, 3, 4, 5) more
Your child has to draw more of the objects shown on the page, count how many there are altogether, and write the answer in the box.

Again, encourage your child to count to reach the answer.

And 1 (2, 3, 4, 5) more
Here, numbers are introduced and replace the objects.

Allow your child to use buttons or fingers if he or she is not confident without them. Build up your child's confidence so he or she is willing to try without the props!

Make use of the number line to help your child with addition.

Read out the words of the activities as this gives meaning to the operation.

If possible, use these examples of adding numbers within the context of your child's daily life: when setting the table, handing out cookies, and so on.

Pages 44 and 45 – Review
Page 44 is a page of sums, on which circles have been given to help with the addition.

Page 45 progresses to use numbers alone, without the help of objects or circles.

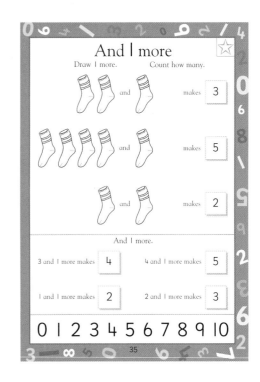

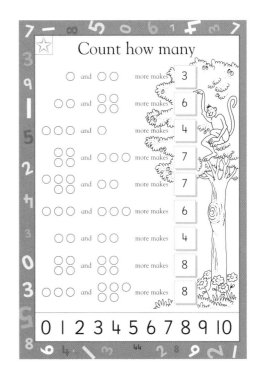

Pages 48, 50, 52, 54, 56 –
1 (2, 3, 4, 5) fewer than

Count how many

Your child has to check the box next to the group that contains one fewer item.

Use a range of vocabulary to help your child understand subtraction—for example, "what is the difference?" or "1 fewer."

Your child may need props to give him or her confidence, but if you have been playing games using practical examples this may not be necessary.

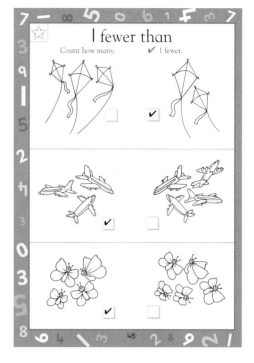

Pages 49, 51, 53, 55, 57 –
Take 1 (2, 3, 4, 5) away

Count how many are left

Your child has to cross out one of the objects and then count how many remain.

The illustration is converted into a problem, so your child can begin to see the connection between practical and abstract uses of numbers.

Encourage your child to color the page before crossing out the objects.

Pages 58 and 59 – Review

Page 58 is a page of activities where your child crosses out 1 or more objects and writes how many remain in the box.

Page 59 is the same process but without the objects.

The number line can help your child. Put a finger or a pencil on the first number and make one hop (or however many hops) backward. The number you land on is the answer. This will help your child work without props.

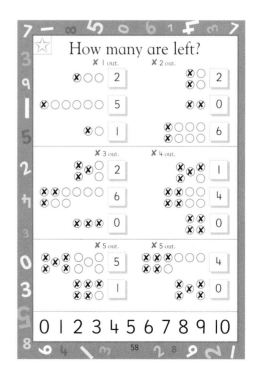

Some answers may be 0 (also nothing or zero). Play games with your child to introduce this concept: "There are two candies and you eat two. How many are left?"

If an entire page is too daunting or confusing for your child, cover some activities with a blank piece of paper. This will enable your child to concentrate on one activity at a time.

Page 60 – Special symbols
The addition sign and the equals sign are introduced.

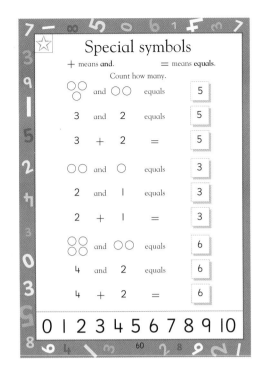

Talk this through with your child, explaining that the signs are used instead of the words, but mean the same thing.

Page 61 – Special symbols
This page introduces the subtraction sign and also uses the equals sign as before.

Your child has to answer the questions, using the symbols and the words. Help your child initially by saying the words aloud.

Page 62 – Now you can do these
A page of addition and subtraction. This page introduces the task of putting the right symbol in the right place. Talk it through with your child, encouraging him or her to choose the correct symbol.

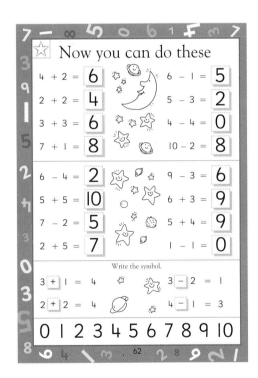

Notes for parents (Pages 64–94)

This section of the book is designed to help your child explore the world of shape, color, measurement, and positional language.

Content

- Pages 64–73 focus on shape and color, and include two review pages.
- Pages 74–83 cover measurement, and include two review pages for measurement, shape, and color.
- Pages 84–91 deal with positional language.
- Pages 92–94 review all the material covered in the section.

How to help your child

These pages are designed for your child to color. This develops pencil control, eye-hand coordination, and concentration. Make sure there is a variety of colored pencils or felt-tip pens available. Crayons are usually too thick for such activities. For writing and drawing, your child will need a sharp, soft pencil.

Talk about the activities on each page and make sure that your child understands what he or she has to do.

Remember this book should be fun as well as educational, so stop before your child loses concentration or becomes restless. This will ensure that your child will want to come back for more!

Page-by-page notes

Introduction to shape and color

By working through the first part of this section, your child will discover the fascinating world of shape and color.

Your child will learn to:
- recognize a circle, a square, a triangle, and a rectangle.
- identify and match these shapes in a variety of contexts.
- draw these shapes.
- recognize colors such as blue, green, red, and yellow.
- recognize the words for shapes and colors.

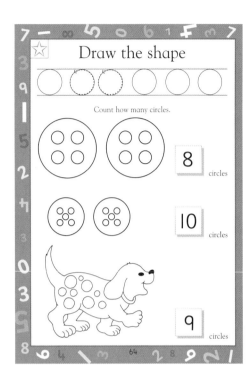

How to help your child

For obvious reasons, this section focuses on flat or plane shapes, but a young child's first experiences will have been with 3-dimensional shapes in the form of bricks, balls, games, etc.

The words *square* and *rectangle* are used to introduce four-sided shapes. They are actually quadrilaterals, but at this stage it is appropriate to use the more familiar words *square* and *rectangle*.

It is not appropriate to introduce angles at this stage. These will be introduced later when your child is at school. However, to help your child keep the lines parallel, you could introduce the drawing of a small square in each corner, a bit like a box. This is the sign that denotes a right angle.

Before attempting the pages, have fun with spotting shapes around the house, or on trips to the stores. Play "I Spy the Shape." Triangles are frequently used within structures as supports and may be difficult to spot.

Collect things that are circles, squares, and rectangles. Let your child feel the shapes. How do they feel? Encourage your child to explain the shapes using the appropriate words. Do they have edges, corners, points, and sides? How many of these do they have?

The four colors introduced are blue, green, red, and yellow. Help your child to identify these colors in his or her environment.

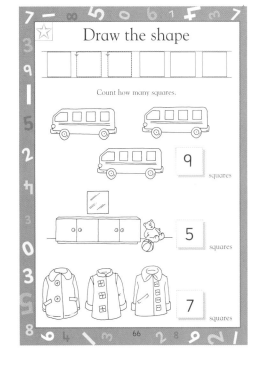

Make collections of things that are the same color, such as red shoes, socks, buttons, and bowls. To help your child read the word for a color, make a label and attach it to an object of that color. Write the word in lower case letters, not capitals.

Your child will probably discover that all greens, for example, are not the same shade or tone. Talk about what your child notices. This can lead to many interesting discoveries about the world of color!

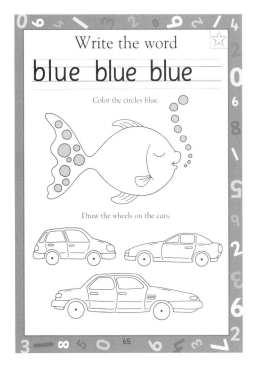

Pages 64, 66, 68, and 70 – Draw the shape

At the top of the first page introducing shapes, your child is familiarized with a shape and is encouraged to draw it.

When drawing a circle (or square, or triangle, or rectangle), make sure your child draws in an anti-clockwise direction. This will help with the formation of letters.

In the task "Count how many" (circles, squares, triangles, or rectangles,) children have to recognize the shapes and then count the number of these shown. When counting, point to each one individually. If your child is unsure, write the numbers out in a line so they can be copied.

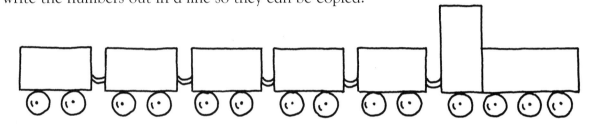

Pages 65, 67, 69, and 71 – Write the word

A color is introduced and children write the word in dots.

In the task "Color the circles" (or squares, triangles, or rectangles), your child not only has to identify the shape but also has to select the right color with which to color the shape.

"Draw a square house (or wheels on the car, a square house, etc.)," is the other task in which your child has to draw the correct shape to complete the picture.

Although the text has been kept to a minimum, there are several words that tell children what to do. Read these out loud with your child, making sure he or she understands what to do.

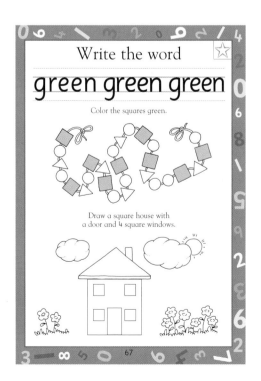

Pages 72–73 – Review

In the task "Match the shapes," the shape on the left has to be matched with the similar ones on the right. Encourage your child to draw a line to the correct shapes, beginning on the left. This reinforces left to right movement, which is necessary for writing.

The task "Color the pattern" reinforces recognition of both shapes and colors by asking the child to color in a pattern.

After completing this section, you and your child can enjoy many activities together, creating shapes and coloring.

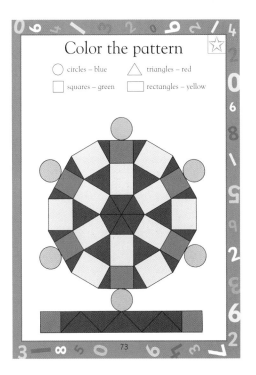

Color the pattern

circles – blue   △ triangles – red

☐ squares – green   ☐ rectangles – yellow

73

Introduction to measurement

This section introduces the early stages of measuring by exploring comparatives. Your child will learn:

- to estimate difference in size.
- the vocabulary needed to compare sizes.

How to help your child

Before doing the activities, collect containers of different sizes and make comparisons between them. Use these words, which are a part of early comparative measuring:

- big, bigger, biggest
- small, smaller, smallest
- long, longer, longest (horizontal measurement in the book)
- taller than / shorter than
- tall, taller, tallest
- short, shorter, shortest
- thick, thicker, thickest
- thin, thinner, thinnest

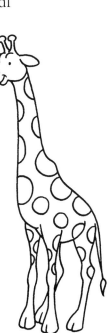

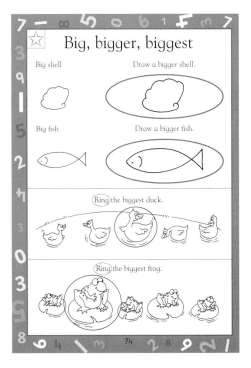

Big, bigger, biggest

Big shell   Draw a bigger shell.

Big fish   Draw a bigger fish.

Ring the biggest duck.

Ring the biggest frog.

74

Pages 74–81 – Measurement

Comparatives are introduced at the top of the page. The tasks include identifying the biggest, smallest etc. by either drawing a ring around the appropriate object or checking the appropriate box. Your child will also draw a bigger shell or fish, a taller flower or bottle, a thicker candle, a thinner balloon etc.

Each page focuses on one of these attributes at a time.

Pages 82–83 – Review

These pages include review exercises on color, shape, and measurement. Your child may need help with understanding what the task involves.

Children can investigate measuring with their own hands and feet, or your hands and feet, before they are introduced to standard measurements.

After completing these pages, your child may become more aware of differences in size (and quantity). Encourage this interest and make it fun. Play measuring games. For example, how many toy cars fit along the edge of the table? How many books tall is a teddy bear?

Introduction to positional language

These words are an important part of a child's language and will be used in a variety of contexts at school. Your child will learn:

- the idea of opposites
- words and their positional meaning, including:
  in front / behind
  inside / outside
  between / beside
  above / on / below
  (The word *below* has been used in this section, but others like *beneath* or *under* are acceptable in order to establish the concept.)

How to help your child

A child gains greater understanding by physically acting out these words. So, before doing these pages, give your child practical experiences.

Play games like "I Spy…" and encourage your child to give you clues and vice versa. Is the object beside the chair? Or is it behind the tree? Play "Simon Says". Ask your child to stand on the mat, between the chairs etc.

Pages 84–85 – In front / Behind

These pages feature a book and a mouse. The tasks require your child to check the box if the book is in front of something or if the mouse is behind something. Make sure your child understands the tasks.

Pages 86–87 – Inside / Outside

Your child has to check the box if the things are inside something, like pennies in a purse, and if things are outside, like the magician's hand. At the bottom of these pages, your child has to draw a circle inside a square and candy outside the jar. This revisits shapes in the context of position and introduces the words *inside* and *outside*.

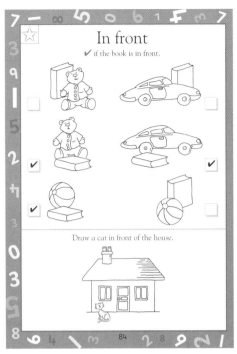

Pages 88–89 – Between / Beside

The first is a drawing page where your child has to draw a ball between toys. Your child also draws shapes between other shapes. The last task revisits shape.

On the next page, your child has to draw things beside a teddy bear. Your child may need help to read the words. The last task again revisits shape.

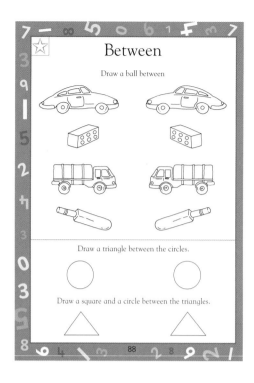

Pages 90–91 – Above, on, and below

These are pages for drawing, counting, and for writing numbers. There are a number of different position words like *over*, *under*, *below*, *beneath*, and *underneath*, so allow your child to use whichever words he or she finds most appropriate, as long as the meaning and the concept are being developed.

Pages 92–93 – Review

These pages review positions in a fun and creative way. Your child has to finish the pictures of a castle and a fairy. The exercise includes counting and writing numbers, and a lot of reading. Make sure your child understands what to do and enjoys doing it!

Page 94 – Review

This fun dot-to-dot page features the shapes your child has learned.

Notes for parents (Pages 95 – 124)

During play activities, children frequently match, sort, create patterns, and talk about sequences. This section of the book reinforces and establishes those concepts and skills in a fun and enjoyable way.

This section of the book includes some counting and number matching, so your child should already be familiar with numbers and quantities up to 10. Shapes and colors are also included in some activities.

Content

By working through this book, your child will learn to:
- look closely at shapes, objects, and patterns.
- match.
- identify similarities and differences.
- sort things into sets.
- use more than one criterion for this sorting process.
- add to sets and count the total.
- recognize what a pattern is.
- continue patterns and create them.
- understand the concept of before and after.
- put events in the right sequential order.
- use ordinal numbers correctly.
- complete sequences.

How to help your child

This section of the book is designed to be an enjoyable experience for both you and your child—a shared time together. Make sure that your child is alert and not too tired. Keep the learning time appropriate to the age and concentration level of your child.

The pages are designed for your child to color, which develops pencil control, eye-hand coordination, and concentration. Make sure there is a variety of colored pencils or felt-tip pens available. Talk about the activities on each page and make sure your child understands what he or she is to do.

How to use this section of the book

Same / Different

Before attempting the first 10 pages of this section of the book, play matching games with your child. Match shoes, socks, plates, or fruit, concentrating on what is the same and what is different about them.

Talk about things that match.

Talk about what is the same and what is different. Encourage your child to notice small differences as well as the obvious ones. For instance, in a collection of leaves, some may be pointed, others may be round, some rough, and others smooth.

This will develop your child's observation skills. Observation skills are helpful in early reading—to differentiate the shapes of letters and how letters contribute to words, and in other curriculum areas such as science and art.

Sorting

Sorting can be practiced with household objects, so make sure that your child has many opportunities to sort objects before doing these pages. Your child can sort toys, clothes, or food items.

Categories or "criteria" have been chosen to make these sorting activities both meaningful and useful in everyday life. The pages introduce various sorting criteria in contexts appropriate for children.

Observation and counting are skills that your child will revisit.

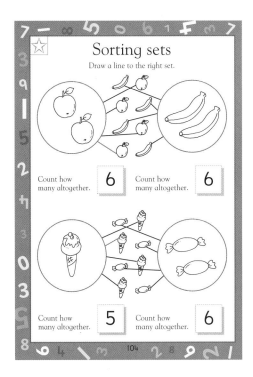

Patterns

Recognizing and creating patterns is an important aspect of a child's development.

Before doing these pages, talk to your child about patterns they see at home. They may be on fabric, wallpaper, kitchenware, or in books.

Let your child copy patterns you have made with buttons, beads, cups, or small toys, and then encourage him or her to make their own patterns. Keep them simple at first, perhaps using just two colors: red button, blue button, red button. As your child becomes more confident, encourage him or her to create more complex patterns.

It is fun to print patterns using corks, small boxes, or fingers and hands.

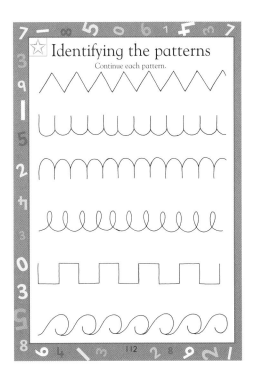

Sequencing

Getting things in the right order can be difficult for a young child.

Give your child the opportunity to experience sequences of events within the context of his or her daily life. Talk about what they do before and after something, and what comes next. Introduce words such as *first*, *second*, and *third*.

Write the numbers 1–10 on cards, mix the cards up, and encourage your child to put them in the right order.

Page-by-page notes

Page 95 – Different

The activity is to encourage your child to find the object that is different.

Your child can then draw a sock and a glove that are different from the ones shown on the page.

Page 96 – Different

This page continues the concept of *different*; the child should by now understand that *different* means "not the same". The child has to draw a ring around the flag that is different, as well as draw the two flags.

Page 97 – Different numbers

This page reinforces the concept of different numbers through the comparison of spots on ladybugs.

Page 98 – Different numbers

Your child can count the shapes on the umbrellas and then draw different numbers on the umbrellas next to them.

Page 99 – The same

Your child has to identify matching animals. Encourage your child to draw a line starting on the left, moving to the right. This reinforces the left to right movement of writing and reading. At the bottom of the page your child can choose the animals they want to draw.

Page 100 – The same

This page introduces the word *pair*. Talk to your child about pairs—two of a kind that go together. In the second activity, your child can draw a pair of shoes.

Page 101 – The same

This page encourages your child to look at both size and shape. If they have not learned to identify colors, they may need your help to complete this task.

They also have to count the number of shapes colored in a specific color.

Page 102 – The same

This is a fun page. Your child has to match the monsters.

Page 103 – The same

Your child has to draw the other half of the monster to match. If it is appropriate, talk to your child about halves. *Half* is introduced in this context as "the other half," which also implies symmetry. Have fun looking for other objects that are symmetrical: buttons and letters, for example. Children can use a mirror to help them draw the other half.

Page 104 – Sorting sets

The word *set* is used instead of *group* because it is a word with which your child should become familiar before starting school.

On this page, the activities involve sorting things into sets—by drawing a line to the appropriate set ring—and counting how many there are in each set.

When your child writes the numbers, make sure that he or she starts at the top and does not retrace.

Page 105 – Adding to sets

Your child should add to the sets by drawing as many more shapes as asked for, and should then count how many in the set.

Page 106 – Sorting the toys

For this activity, there are two set rings, one with wheeled toys and the other with toys without wheels. Talk to your child about the toys in the sets. What do they notice? They are all toys, but what is the difference between the two sets? What is the same about the toys in each set?

After you have talked about what your child notices, encourage them to do the sorting. An example is given for each set.

Page 107 – Sorting the trees

For this task, your child has to sort the trees according to the number of apples on them. Count how many of each type of tree. Your child has to draw an additional tree with the requisite number of apples. Now count how many of each type of tree including those drawn by the child.

Page 108 – Sorting the animals

In this activity your child has to sort the animals according to the number of legs they have and draw a line to the right part of the Ark.
An example is shown.

Page 109 – Sorting the animals

This time the animals with the specified number of legs have to be ringed.

Page 110 – Sorting the fish

This is both a sorting and a matching activity. Your child has to look at the number on each fish and match that fish to the fisherman wearing that number. The child should draw a fishing line for each fish that matches.

Page 111 – Sorting the fish

This is also a sorting and matching activity. Your child has to look closely at the patterns on the fish and match each fish to the fisherman wearing a hat with the same pattern. The child should draw a fishing line for each fish that matches. Children may use a different color for each number.

At the bottom of the page the child has to count how many fish of each pattern there are.

Page 112 – Identifying patterns

This page encourages your child to identify simple patterns that have been started for them. Left to right movement is important. The first four patterns are the basis for letters.

Page 113 – Identifying patterns

Your child has to complete patterns and create his or her own.

This activity can be extended beyond the book and your child can decorate his or her own paper plates.

Page 114 – Identifying patterns

Again your child has to complete the patterns. The pattern is simple but make sure your child really looks at the items; some involve counting and one involves shape orientation.

Page 115 – Identifying patterns

These are more complex, so make sure your child understands what has to be done!

Page 116 – In the right order

This page relates to a child's world and what they do before and after something.

Talk about the pictures before your child puts the check marks in the boxes. Also talk about the pictures illustrating first, second, and third before completing the boxes.

Page 117 – In the right order

The activities involve three pictures. Your child has to decide what comes first, second, or third in the sequence of events.

Talk about the pictures before your child completes the task.

Page 118 – Identifying patterns

Your child has to complete the sequence of numbers by drawing the missing objects.

If your child finds it difficult to count by twos, he or she need some help with the last activity.

Page 119 – The missing numbers

In these activities there is more than one missing number.

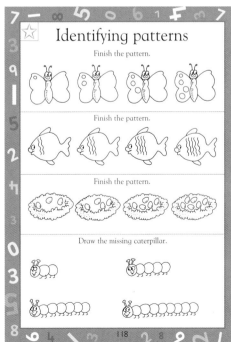

Page 120 – Mary sorted her snails

Your child will have fun matching, looking for patterns, and looking for similarities and differences in Mary's garden.

Children have to sort the different kinds of snails, draw them in the circles given, and count how many snails there are in each circle.

Page 121 – Mary grew some flowers

This page is both an exercise in matching and in looking for similarities and differences.

Page 122 – The maze

Your child has to follow the pattern sequence to find his or her way out of the maze.

Page 123 – Dot-to-dot

By finishing the pattern and completing the dot-to-dot your child will produce lovely pictures.

At the bottom of the page the child can draw his or her own dot-to-dot pattern.

Page 124 – Different

Your child has to identify the animals that are the same and draw a ring around the animal that is different.

At the bottom of the page your child can draw two different animals. Talk about their choices.